Thriving Beyond the Early Years

Thriving Beyond the Early Years

Transitioning from Professional to Master Teacher

Matthew J. Jennings

ROWMAN & LITTLEFIELD
Lanham • Boulder • New York • London

Published by Rowman & Littlefield
An imprint of The Rowman & Littlefield Publishing Group, Inc.
4501 Forbes Boulevard, Suite 200, Lanham, Maryland 20706
www.rowman.com
86–90 Paul Street, London EC2A 4NE

Copyright © 2021 by Matthew J. Jennings

All rights reserved. No part of this book may be reproduced in any form or by any electronic or mechanical means, including information storage and retrieval systems, without written permission from the publisher, except by a reviewer who may quote passages in a review.

British Library Cataloguing in Publication Information Available

Library of Congress Cataloging-in-Publication Data
Names: Jennings, Matthew, author.
Title: Thriving beyond the early years : transitioning from professional to master teacher / Matthew Jennings.
Description: Lanham : Rowman and Littlefield,, [2021] | Includes bibliographical references. |
Summary: "This book provides the research-based strategies teachers need to successfully implement learning activities"— Provided by publisher.
Identifiers: LCCN 2021029526 (print) | LCCN 2021029527 (ebook) | ISBN 9781475862423 (cloth) | ISBN 9781475862430 (paperback) | ISBN 9781475862447 (ebook)
Subjects: LCSH: Teachers—In-service training—United States. | Teachers—Professional relationships—United States. | Mentoring in education—United States.
Classification: LCC LB1731 .J395 2021 (print) | LCC LB1731 (ebook) | DDC 370.71/1—dc23
LC record available at https://lccn.loc.gov/2021029526
LC ebook record available at https://lccn.loc.gov/2021029527

Table of Contents

Acknowledgments — vii

1 Introduction — 1
2 Teacher-Guided Discussions — 9
3 Structured Small-Group Discussions — 41
4 Student-Led Small-Group Discussions — 53
5 D.E.E.P. Learning Tasks — 61

Study Guide — 85
Appendix — 91
References — 95
About the Author — 97

Acknowledgments

I want to thank my wife, MaryAnn Jennings, for her help with the formatting of this text. I would also like to thank my daughter, Tara Jennings, for her proofreading and revision suggestions. Lastly, I would like to thank Jennifer Ward, Lisa Ventura, and Melissa Jennings for their content suggestions. Without the help from each of you, this book would not have reached the desired level of quality.

Chapter 1

Introduction

Imagine learning that you have a serious health condition that can be corrected through surgery. While complex, the surgery is typically a safe procedure. Upon arriving to the hospital, you learn that the doctor performing the surgery will be a first-year resident that recently graduated from medical school. You feel no comfort when the chief surgeon tells you that everything will be alright because the resident is very motivated, loves to cut, and really wants to be successful with the operation.

Imagine another scenario. You have a complex legal issue with the potential for a critical outcome. The firm that you have been working with decides to assign your case to a recent law school graduate. This eager lawyer will be the only attorney that will handle your case. Would you find yourself thinking that things will be okay because they are licensed to practice law?

Fortunately, both of these scenarios are highly improbable. The reason this is improbable is that professions other than education understand the importance of experience. Typically, they assign responsibilities based upon the knowledge and experience of the individual professionals. Professions such as law and medicine recognize that while a basic level of knowledge and skill is necessary to practice the profession, expertise is developed through structured experiences over time.

Contrast this to the teaching profession. A recent graduate of a teacher education program will be expected to perform the same responsibilities as a veteran teacher. Typically, they will be evaluated with the same instrument and, with the exception of orientation and some degree of mentoring, will likely receive the same professional development.

If teachers entered the profession completely prepared to independently handle a classroom with the same expertise as experienced teachers, this scenario would make sense. Yet, we know that teachers in their first few years are usually not as effective in achieving student learning as more experienced colleagues. As good as any teacher preparation program may be, accepting responsibility for independently teaching a group of students requires a somewhat steep learning curve.

Teachers in the first few years in the classroom have unique professional development needs. In my book *From First Year to First Rate* (Jennings, 2021a), I identify those needs and provide the knowledge and skills novice teachers need to master. In *Transforming Novices to Professionals* (Jennings, 2021b), I describe a four-year process districts can use to facilitate novice teachers' proficiency with these foundational components of effective teaching.

This book is focused on further developing teacher knowledge and skills so they can move from the professional to the master level of teaching. A professional teacher is proficient in classroom management, direct instruction, and high-quality classroom assessment. A master teacher is proficient in these areas but is also capable of competently going beyond them to use strategies that promote deep learning of critical content. To promote deep learning with students requires an understanding of the four different levels of knowledge.

FOUR LEVELS OF KNOWLEDGE

Declarative knowledge is the "what" of school subject areas. More specifically, it is the facts, details, and terms that form the foundation of all academic disciplines. In mathematics, multiplication facts and definitions of geometric shapes are examples of declarative knowledge. In language arts, parts of speech and definitions of story elements are examples. All subject areas have a significant body of declarative knowledge that must be memorized. In addition, the retrieval of this information must be become automatic. If students lack fluency with the retrieval of declarative knowledge, they will not have the cognitive capacity necessary for more complex cognitive tasks.

Procedural knowledge is the "how" of school subject areas. It is the application of declarative knowledge in predictable, routine, and conventional ways. In mathematics, completing double-digit multiplication problems and determining the surface area of a given shape are examples of procedural knowledge. In language arts, using knowledge of phonics to sound out a word and using knowledge of mechanics to edit a paper are examples of procedural knowledge. Most declarative knowledge has rules or procedures associated with its use. Therefore, students need to know these procedures and follow them accurately.

Declarative and procedural knowledge are the foundation for developing expert levels of understanding in any content area. Yet, these two types of knowledge are insufficient by themselves. Emerging expertise in any domain of study requires conditional and conceptual knowledge.

Conditional knowledge is the "when" of the use of content knowledge. This type of knowledge involves deciding on the appropriateness of the use of various types of procedural knowledge. In other words, conditional knowledge enables students to know how to select the most appropriate, efficient, and effective approach from a range of possible methods. In mathematics, knowing when it is appropriate to use estimation strategies is an example of conditional knowledge. In language arts, knowing when it is sufficient to skim a section of text would also be an example of conditional knowledge. Experts in any subject area have a wide range of strategies at their disposal, and they know which one to use in a given situation.

Conceptual knowledge is the "why" of the use of declarative knowledge. Having conceptual knowledge enables students to understand why they are doing what they are doing. For example, in mathematics, understanding the relationship between the mean, median, and mode of a given data is an example of conceptual knowledge. In language arts, understanding how similes, metaphors, and personification are similar and different is an additional example of conceptual knowledge. Conceptual knowledge is necessary for functioning at the metacognitive level. Without conceptual knowledge, learners are not able to make strategic decisions about the ways in which they apply information to solving a range of complex problems.

THE CASE FOR "DEEPER" LEARNING

If educators seek to promote long-term retention and the positive transfer of learning to future situations, then all four of these types of knowledge are critically important. As students move through each level of knowledge, their retention of everything learned at previous levels is solidified. Declarative knowledge is reinforced through the application of procedural knowledge and the use of conditional knowledge reinforces both procedural and declarative knowledge. The use of conceptual knowledge reinforces all three levels.

A factor that educators must consider when designing instruction is the similarity between the situations in which something is learned and to which we seek to have that learning transfer. The more similar the two situations, the more learning will transfer from one to the other (Hunter, 1971). Knowing that similarity generates transfer, if we want to maximize transfer of knowledge for future use, then we must make the two learning situations as similar as possible. In other words, if we want students to use the knowledge they are taught in the contexts they will need to use it, then we must provide similar types of experiences through classroom instruction.

Unfortunately, most of the learning in school remains at the declarative and procedural level. As students progress through grades, they continue to pile up more and more disconnected bits of information, algorithms, techniques, and methods without connecting them to accomplish the broader goals they were intended for (Conley, 2014). Our students end up possessing knowledge without purpose and engage in activity without meaning. Thus, our need to reteach and review what we thought our students had already learned should come as no surprise.

Not all methods of teaching are equally suited for facilitating acquisition of each level of knowledge. Direct, explicit instruction is the most effective and efficient way to teach basic concepts, terms, and the application of content to accomplish basic routines and tasks (Clark, Kirschner, & Sweller, 2012). However, direct instruction is not equally as effective for facilitating student understanding at the conditional and conceptual levels. Learning at these levels of knowledge requires tasks that create opportunities for students to give material significance, personalize it, incorporate it into their experience, and imbue it with their own interpretation and value (Barron & Darling-Hammond, 2008).

For some time, there has been debate in education over the use of direct instruction versus inquiry-based approaches to learning. Instead of viewing this as an either/or proposition, educators must view this as an "and" situation. Explicit, direct instruction is necessary at the beginning of a learning sequence, but it should be gradually faded out as student's knowledge and skills increase. If the content is appropriate, then the teacher must extend the learning with activities that require the deep learning characteristic of work at the conditional and conceptual knowledge levels.

Not all topics of study are suitable or even desirable for this type of deep learning. There is no need for critical or creative thinking with basic additional facts or the correct spelling of given words. However, for every standard that is identified as being at the core of the discipline, students must engage in high-quality deep learning tasks. In other words, for the content standards deemed essential for future use, whether that use is in academics, the workplace, or life in general, students must have the opportunity to engage in tasks that require critical and creative thinking. Only then will they have the greatest probability of retaining and using that knowledge successfully.

Optimally, curriculum decisions about what is and is not a priority will be made by teams of teachers responsible for instructing the same subject area. This encourages consistency of intended learning outcomes across classrooms and schools within a district. Minimally, inconsistency with the content of instruction yields gaps in prior knowledge. Future teachers cannot count on student's coming to their classrooms with the necessary prior knowledge when such gaps exist.

HOW TEACHERS CAN PROMOTE "DEEPER" LEARNING

Much like the novice learner must first develop declarative and procedural knowledge, the novice teacher must develop proficiency with the basics of teaching before attempting to become skilled with more advanced instructional methodologies. The foundation for all teaching is proficiency with classroom management, direct instruction, and valid, reliable classroom assessment.

A teacher cannot provide high-quality instruction in a chaotic environment. Likewise, a teacher cannot make high-quality instruction decisions without acquiring and using high-quality student performance data. Furthermore, a teacher cannot effectively and efficiently promote understanding of essential declarative and procedural knowledge without being able to provide high-quality direct instruction.

If a teacher does not demonstrate proficiency with classroom management, direct instruction, and classroom assessment, then those should serve as the focus for their continuing professional development. This should remain the focus of their professional development until they achieve proficiency or separate from the profession. However, those who have demonstrated this proficiency are ready to learn the what, why, and how of engaging students in deep learning tasks. This will be the focus for the remainder of this text.

Two advanced instructional strategies are the focus of subsequent chapters. The first is disciplined academic discussions and the second is D.E.E.P. learning tasks. Disciplined academic discussions differ from recitations in which the teacher asks a question, students respond, and the teacher evaluates that response. This cycle of initiate, respond, and evaluate is primarily used to check for student understanding. Disciplined academic discussions are a process through which students give voice to their thoughts in a disciplined manner, as they interact with others to make meaning and advance both individual and collective understanding of a topic.

The second instructional strategy is "D.E.E.P." learning tasks. D.E.E.P. learning tasks differ from activities assigned for students to achieve summative closure with a topic. Creating a poster summarizing the key points of a unit of study or using units of measurement to measure one's room at home requires applying what has been learned to provide a correct answer. In comparison, D.E.E.P. learning tasks present students with authentic problems that have multiple solutions. These solutions are "correct" if they can be justified on the basis of sound evidence and reasoning. These are the types of tasks professionals engage in through their vocations on a regular basis.

Disciplined academic discussions and D.E.E.P. learning tasks can be combined as part of an instructional sequence, but they do not have to be. Disciplined academic discussions frequently serve as an excellent tool for building the knowledge required to complete a D.E.E.P. learning task. However, some tasks do not lend themselves to one or the other of these instructional strategies. Thus, they can be used independent of one another.

These two strategies were selected for several reasons. First, as you will see in subsequent chapters, the effectiveness of both of these types of learning activities is supported by a solid, growing body of evidence. Second, both strategies work equally well in all content areas with various types of students and with adjustments at various grade levels. Third, these strategies are not costly to learn and implement. They do not require resources beyond that which most teachers already have at their disposal.

On the other hand, disciplined academic discussions and D.E.E.P. learning tasks are two strategies that are challenging to master. Effective use of these strategies requires deliberate and focused practice. In addition, the nature of these strategies requires teachers to accept a change in their role from that of the primary information provider to a facilitator of students learning. If our goal is to promote long-term retention of core concepts and the transfer of knowledge to similar future situations, then this is a challenge worth accepting.

Ideally every student would have a teacher capable of promoting deep learning with their students. Yet, for most inexperienced teachers, this is likely implausible. It takes structured and deliberate practice with high-quality feedback to master the foundational aspects of teaching. Without these foundational aspects, promoting deep learning will be very difficult if not impossible. This process can be accelerated through providing comprehensive, structured, sequenced growth opportunities, but no matter what is done, becoming a highly effective teacher takes time.

This book is intended to provide the content necessary for continued professional growth to teachers at the point in their careers where they have achieved proficiency with the foundational aspects of teaching. This is not to be confused with the number of years of experience a teacher has acquired. One can teach for many years and not achieve significant professional growth. Having one year of experience multiple times does not lead to becoming a master teacher.

In chapter 1, the focus will be learning how to conduct teacher-guided discussions. Chapter 3 is intended to build upon chapter 2 by adding a variety of structured small-group discussion protocols. Chapter 4 focuses on implementation of student-led discussion groups. Chapter 5 will focus on designing, implementing, and assessing student projects that are designed to encourage deep learning of critical content.

The sequencing of these chapter topics is purposeful. They represent a progression from the easiest to the most challenging instructional strategies to design, implement, and evaluate. Thus, if given the choice, focus should be on developing proficiency with teacher-guided discussions as the first step. This topic is the subject of the next chapter.

Chapter 2

Teacher-Guided Discussions

Think about the powerful learning experiences you have had in your life. Who did the majority of the thinking and talking needed to create those experiences? Was it your instructor or was it you in concert with other learners? There is a high probability that at least in part, your most powerful learning experiences came from the construction of ideas built through talking and listening to other learners. If this is the case, you are not alone. A growing body of research supports the fact that questioning and discussion are both an important means and ends of student learning.

In his meta-analysis of instructional strategies related to student achievement, John Hattie (2008) determined that classroom discussion is a high-impact instructional strategy. More specifically, he concluded that the typical student engaged in classroom discussion could achieve two years of academic growth in a one-year time period. However, Hattie specified that these benefits only occur if the strategy is used effectively.

Other researchers have connected student engagement through questioning and discussion to improved learning outcomes, including higher levels of thinking and increased student achievement (Applebee, 2003; Murphy, Wilkinson, Soter, Hennessy, & Alexander, 2009). Furthermore, the skills of questioning and discussion are valuable in the workplace (Wagner, 2010) and in higher education (Conley, 2008).

Given that discussion is an evidence-based instructional strategy, it could be assumed that it is a prevalent practice in classrooms. However, researchers find that true academic discussion is rarely present in today's K–12 classrooms. According to Kamil et al. (2008), discussion currently accounts for an average of only 1.7 minutes per 60 minutes of classroom instruction. The Learning 24/7 study of 1,500 classrooms found evidence of academic dialogue and discussion in only .5 percent of classrooms observed (Schmoker, 2007).

Interestingly, Applebee (2003) found that middle and high school teachers report the use of discussion as their primary instructional format. Yet, in studying 112 eighth- and ninth-grade language arts classes, it was found that students engaged in less than one minute of true discussion per hour of class. Thus, based on available research, one can conclude that discussion is a potentially high-impact instructional strategy that teachers falsely perceive they are using regularly.

When classroom talk between teachers and students does occur, it is typically a sequence involving a teacher asking a question, a student responding, and then the teacher evaluating the quality of that response. In fact, teachers repeat this pattern approximately 300–400 times per day, asking as many as 120 questions per hour (Vogler, 2008). This pattern of questioning is valuable early in the learning cycle for checking student understanding. However, no matter how frequently it occurs, student's response of a correct answer to a teacher's question does not promote the analysis, evaluation, and synthesis necessary for deep learning to occur.

Because it improves comprehension of content, discussion with peers should occur regularly throughout the learning cycle. However, while talking about content helps students grasp concepts and understand tasks, most classroom discussions do little to spur students' critical thinking (Murphy et al., 2009). By itself, increasing the quantity of student talk-time does not help them perform tasks such as analyzing writers' claims, evaluating the coherence of arguments, or developing and defending their own arguments. Deep learning requires students to engage in critical analytical talk (Goodwin, 2014).

Critical analytical talk requires consideration of open-ended questions at the upper end of Bloom's taxonomy. In addition, this type of talk requires the use of multiple sources of information and evidence to support responses (Murphy et al., 2009). Providing the right type of questions and considering multiple sources of information are essential but they are not enough. For students to develop critical thinking skills, they must receive direct instruction in identifying assumptions, analyzing and evaluating arguments, and using the appropriate communication skills. What follows is a series of steps teachers can use to plan, facilitate, and evaluate teacher-guided discussions that promote students' critical thinking.

TEACHER AND STUDENT PREPARATION

Preparation for teacher-guided discussions involves five steps. First, the teacher must ensure that the emotional and social climate in the classroom supports the open exchange of ideas. Second, the teacher must decide upon the most appropriate seating arrangement for students. Third, the teacher must develop a question or set of questions he or she will use to launch and guide the discussion. Fourth, the teacher must identify and assign preparation work for student completion. Lastly, the teacher needs to identify the student discussion skills he or she will teach and have students reflect upon. This section will address each step of preparation tor teacher-guided discussion in the order stated.

Classroom norms

Suppose you were at a faculty meeting and someone made a sarcastic comment that embarrassed you. At the time you did not have a good response to this comment. A half hour later, you are driving home, and you are annoyed with yourself because you can suddenly think of many different comebacks you wish you had said. Why does this happen?

The human brain responds to sensory input in a hierarchy. The top priority for our attention is anything that relates to survival. The next highest priority of input is that which generates strong emotion. The lowest priority for our attention is cognition. When we experience sensory input at a higher level, it becomes very difficult to focus our attention at a lower level in the hierarchy. Thus, when we experience a strong emotional response, we are unable to perform higher-level thinking. In the aforementioned example, you could not perform the cognitive activity of thinking of a witty response because you felt the emotion of embarrassment. You could not think clearly until you felt safe in your car and you were out of the situation that was causing you embarrassment.

In some recitation-based classrooms, many students are so concerned about being called upon by the teacher that they have tremendous difficulty focusing on the information being provided. The fear of embarrassment due to not having the correct answer is so great that they simply cannot focus their attention on the content of the lecture. This is especially problematic when the teacher responds sarcastically or harshly to incorrect responses. This hierarchical relationship between emotion and cognition has significant implications for how teachers lead discussions.

If teachers are to lead meaningful discussions, they must create a classroom climate conducive to that goal. Genuine collaboration cannot occur in a hostile environment. It must be a climate in which the risk-taking associated with sharing thoughts is encouraged and respected. Furthermore, there must be mutual respect for a diversity of ideas and value for the contributions made by all students. A starting point for creating this type of classroom environment is teaching and reinforcing norms for disciplined academic discussions.

Even though different forms of discussion require different norms for participation, there are some norms that are universal to all disciplined academic discussions. While the following list is neither exhaustive nor is it necessarily appropriate for your students, examples to consider include the following:

- Allow the speaker to finish his or her thought.
- Embrace silence as an opportunity for thinking.
- When possible, incorporate others' comments into your response.
- Control the emotional intensity of your statements.
- Make sure your nonverbal signals demonstrate respect for the speaker.
- Ask questions to seek clarification.
- Monitor your talk in order to avoid monopolizing the conversation.
- Talk to each other and not just the teacher.
- Seek to build ideas and develop an understanding instead of trying to win.

Neither do students automatically understand the reasons for these norms nor do they put them into practice with ease. The important point is that students must be explicitly taught the reasons for the norms selected. Then they must engage in intentional practice with these norms, followed with opportunities for reflection and feedback.

Classroom seating

Another consideration related to the classroom environment is the arrangement of classroom seating. Restructuring the environment helps students get into the right mindset for discussion. The seating arrangement serves as the cue for the type of thinking, listening, and speaking students are expected to do. Thus, if the goal is for students to speak to each other, then we need to make sure they can all see one another. Therefore, the optimal arrangement of desks or chairs is a circular or U-shaped formation. This is not always possible given the constraints some teachers encounter, but it is worth doing if it can be done.

The following scale is designed to assist the reader in determining how well they are currently creating an environment conducive to classroom discussions. The scale begins with a question and is followed by a statement of the standard. The teacher and student evidence are examples of what this standard looks like in practice. The rating scales describe developmental levels of the use of the standard. The reader should review the information in this and the subsequent scales presented throughout the chapter and then make an assessment of his or her current use of this instructional strategy. Near the conclusion of this section, a compilation of all of the scores will be completed. This will serve as the basis for action planning to improve application of classroom discussion skills.

SELF-RATING OF CLASSROOM DISCUSSION ENVIRONMENT

How does the social, emotional, and physical climate of the classroom support discussion?	
The teacher uses strategies to create a social, emotional, and physical climate conducive to classroom discussion.	
Teacher Evidence: • Norms encouraging sharing of thoughts and respect for a diversity of ideas are established. • Classroom discussions begin with review of the expected norms. • The teacher appropriately addresses violations of established norms. • The student seating arrangement is conducive to the discussion goals.	**Student Evidence:** • Student behavior demonstrates understanding of the established discussion norms. • When asked, students can identify the classroom discussion norms and explain the rationale for these norms.

	Innovating (4.0)	*Applying (3.0)*	*Developing (2.0)*	*Beginning (1.0)*
Classroom Discussion Environment	My use of this standard is creative enough to be shared with other faculty members so they can use it with their students.	I use explicit strategies to teach and reinforce classroom discussion norms and I arrange the classroom seating to meet discussion goals.	I attempt to create a classroom environment conductive to discussion, but the results of my attempts are frequently ineffective.	I have made minimal effort to create a classroom environment conducive to classroom discussions.

Focus questions

Creating appropriate high-quality questions in advance is another key role the teacher must play. Lower-level cognitive questions seeking to promote recall or comprehension of material previously taught by the teacher are valuable. These types of questions assist students in committing knowledge to memory. They are even more valuable with students in the primary grades (Walsh & Sattes, 2005).

Higher-level cognitive questions seeking to have students mentally manipulate information previously learned in order to create an answer or to support an answer with logically reasoned evidence are also valuable. In addition to promoting long-term retention of information, these questions help students develop critical thinking skills.

On average, during classroom recitations, approximately 60 percent of the questions asked are at the lower cognitive level. Of the remaining 40 percent, 20 percent are procedural and 20 percent are at the higher cognitive level (Cotton, 1988). Importantly, researchers have found that increasing the use of higher-level cognitive questions to considerably above 20 percent produces superior learning gains for students above the primary grades and especially for secondary students (Walsh & Sattes, 2005).

Thus, it is not that one type of question is better than the other. Instead, both types of questions serve an instructional purpose. Teachers must understand their instructional goals and then match the type of questions asked to the level of thinking desired. Early in a learning cycle, a high incidence of lower-level cognitive questions that elicit correct responses is appropriate. Later in the learning cycle, the balance must switch to an emphasis on higher-level questions: the types that are the heart of disciplined academic discussions.

Higher-level questions meeting certain criteria serve as the catalyst for the type of student thinking that leads to purposeful listening and speaking. Quality focus questions have a clear purpose, focus on critical content, are asked at the correct cognitive level, and are worded clearly. Often one carefully prepared focus question that meets these criteria is enough to serve as the launching point for an academic classroom discussion.

The purpose of the focus question depends upon the instructional objective. In discussion, we seek to challenge students to think about concepts and formulate personal responses. Thus, to be effective, the question must engage students personally and emotionally. Without student interest and attention, it is probable they will not put forth the effort to engage in deep discussion.

In addition to engaging students personally and emotionally, discussion questions are intended to encourage students to make connections that will help them move information to long-term memory. Therefore, we must consider the content we seek to promote long-term retention of. Quality focus questions address content essential to the topic under study. Furthermore, because all students must possess the breadth and depth of knowledge required to think about the issue, the question must logically and directly build upon previous questions asked throughout the unit of study.

Focus questions for discussions must encourage students to speculate, formulate hypotheses, and offer evidence to support their ideas. Therefore, they must be open-ended, inviting multiple perspective or points of view. If a question can be answered yes or no, then it is not a high-quality focus question for a discussion. Thus, questions written for academic discussions need to be written at the analysis, evaluation, or synthesis level of Bloom's taxonomy.

In order to accomplish any of these objectives, the question must be written clearly. This requires that the vocabulary used is appropriate for the age of the students as well as the content being studied. The words used to phrase the question must be unambiguous and precise. Lastly, the question should use the fewest possible words and the simplest possible sentence structure. The following are examples of high-quality focus questions:

- Should animals be used for scientific testing?
- Is human activity responsible for global climate change?
- Should the United States continue to use the Electoral College to determine the presidency?
- Are social networking sites good for our society?
- In *The Call of the Wild*, what was London trying to say about society at that time?
- In *The Lord of the Flies*, does Golding seem to be advocating for or against a structured society?
- What is a number?
- Do quadratic and cubic equations always have a solution?

As part of the process of crafting focus questions, it is wise to take the time to anticipate student responses. Anticipating logical and plausible lines of reasoning and potentially erroneous thinking is a good check of the quality of the question. If the question would not produce a range of perspectives, it is unlikely to serve as the catalyst to a robust discussion. In addition, anticipating potential student responses helps the teachers plan effective steps they may need to take in order to sustain or help students modify their thinking.

SELF-RATING OF FOCUS QUESTION DEVELOPMENT

Do I develop an effective focus question or questions for discussions?	
The teacher prepares an effective focus question or questions for discussions.	
Teacher Evidence: • The question or questions focus on content that is essential to the topic under study. • The question or questions are open-ended and encourage multiple perspectives. • The question or questions are worded clearly. • The question or questions logically and directly build upon previously introduced content. • It is evident that the teacher has anticipated potential student responses and planned accordingly.	**Student Evidence:** • Student responses indicate understanding of the focus question or questions. • Students demonstrate high levels of personal engagement with the content of the focus question or questions.

(Continued)

(Continued)

	Innovating (4.0)	Applying (3.0)	Developing (2.0)	Beginning (1.0)
Focus Question(s) Development	My use of this standard is creative enough to be shared with other faculty members so they can use it with their students.	I create focus questions that have a clear purpose, focus on critical content, are asked at the higher levels of Bloom's taxonomy, and are worded clearly.	I attempt to create a focus question or questions, but the results of my attempts are frequently ineffective.	I have made minimal effort to prepare a focus question or questions for discussion.

Student preparation

Another essential role related to creating a focus question or questions that must be completed in advance is planning activities designed to prepare students for the discussion. Students need to have enough content in their heads to talk about as well as enough language to express that content. This preparation can take several different forms.

An assignment students can do in preparation for a classroom discussion is reading from text or primary sources. Careful selection of readings that are provided to students in advance results in common grounds for discussion. Prior to reading, students should be taught the meaning of words that could impede understanding of the text. This should be done efficiently and does not require review of every challenging word, only those that could impede student comprehension.

In addition, the teacher should establish a purpose for the reading assignment. Students will read with greater comprehension when given a clear, analytic, or provocative purpose for their reading. Often, this is done in the form of a question or a prompt.

As students read the text, they should make annotations they can refer to during the discussion. This is a process that must be both taught and modeled repeatedly for students. Common annotations include the following:

- Underlining major points
- Placing a star, asterisk, or other symbol in the margin to emphasize important statements

- Vertical lines in the margin to denote longer statements that are too long to be underlined
- Numbers in the margin to indicate a sequence of points made by the author in development of an argument
- Numbers of other pages in the margin to indicate where else in the text the author makes the same point
- Circling confusing words or phrases
- Writing in the margin, or at the top or bottom of the page to record questions.

The text and these annotations support student discussion by providing points of reference for their thinking and accountability for their points of view.

Another assignment option that can be provided to students in advance is independent research on topics related to the discussion. Independent research of a topic prior to discussion will yield a diversity of viewpoints. Of course, the quality of the sources students use for their research is critical. This option requires students to have the ability to evaluate the credibility of information sources.

Lastly, students can complete written assignments or generate questions prior to the discussion. Written assignments help students clarify their thinking in advance. Student-generated questions yield similar outcomes with the added bonus of preparing students to ask questions during the discussion. Regardless of the form of preparation, all discussants should be required to complete activities that prepare them to respond to the focus question or questions that will be posed.

Communication and reasoning skills

Another necessity teachers must prepare for when planning to lead classroom discussions is direct instruction on communication and reasoning skills. Unless students know how to listen effectively, they cannot fully understand the ideas of other discussion members. Likewise, without effective speaking skills, they will not be able to clearly communicate the ideas they are trying to contribute to the conversation. The following is a list of potential mini-lesson topics for speaking and listening organized by grade level. In this table, the I is for the introduction of the content, R is for review and extension, and M is for when it is expected that students will demonstrate proficient use of the skill. Mini-lessons on these topics should occur with increasing sophistication in the grade levels designated in the chart.

K–5 Speaking and listening skills for classroom discussions						
Skill	K	1	2	3	4	5
Take turns speaking about topics under discussion.	I	R	M			
Continue conversations through multiple exchanges.	I	R	M			
Ask and answer questions to clarify something that is not understood.	I	R	M			
Speak audibly.	I	R	M			
Remain on topic.	I	R	M			
Express thoughts, feelings, and ideas clearly.	I	R	M			
Build on others' talk in conversations by responding to the comments of others.		I	R	M		
Speak in complete sentences.		I	R	M		
Link comments to those made by others.			I	R	M	
Ask questions about what a speaker said in order to gain additional information or deepen understanding of a topic.			I	R	M	
Draw on preparation and other information known about the topic to explore ideas under discussion.				I	R	M
Identify the reasons and evidence a speaker provides in order to support particular points.					I	R
Carry out assigned roles (small-group discussions).					I	R
Review the key ideas expressed and draw conclusions in light of information and knowledge gained from the discussion.						I
Summarize the points a speaker makes and explain how each claim is supported by reasons and evidence.						I
6–12 Speaking and listening skills for classroom discussions					
---	---	---	---	---	---
Skill	6	7	8	9–10	11–12
Carry out assigned roles (small-group discussions).	M				
Identify the reasons and evidence a speaker provides in order to support particular points.	M				
Review the key ideas expressed and draw conclusions in light of information and knowledge gained from the discussion.	R	M			
Summarize the points a speaker makes and explain how each claim is supported by reasons and evidence.	R	M			

6–12 Speaking and listening skills for classroom discussions

Skill	6	7	8	9–10	11–12
Demonstrate understanding of multiple perspectives through reflection and paraphrasing.	I	R	M		
Delineate a speaker's argument and specific claims	I	R	M		
Distinguish claims that are supported by reasons and evidence from claims that are not.	I	R	M		
Present claims and findings, sequencing ideas logically and using pertinent descriptions, facts, and details to accentuate main ideas or themes.	I	R	M		
Set specific goals and deadlines for small-group discussions.	I	R	M		
Track progress toward goals and deadlines for small-group discussions.		I	R	M	
Acknowledge new information expressed by others and, when warranted, modify one's own views.		I	R	M	
Evaluate the soundness of the reasoning and the relevance and sufficiency of the evidence for a speaker's argument.		I	R	M	
Pose questions that connect the ideas of several speakers.			I	R	M
Respond to others' questions and comments with relevant evidence, observations, and ideas.			I	R	M
Identify when the speaker introduces fallacious reasoning and exaggerated or distorted evidence.			I	R	M
In small groups, follow rules for making decisions.			I	R	M
Relate the current discussion to broader themes or ideas.				I & R	M
Actively involve others in the discussion.				I & R	M
Clarify, verify, or challenge ideas and conclusions of others.				I & R	M
Summarize points of agreement and disagreement.				I & R	M
Promote divergent and creative perspectives.				I & R	M

(Continued)

(Continued)

6–12 Speaking and listening skills for classroom discussions					
Skill	6	7	8	9–10	11–12
Synthesize comments, claims, and evidence on all sides of an issue, resolving contradictions when possible.				I & R	M
Determine when additional information or research is required to deepen the investigation or complete the task.				I & R	M
Convey a clear and distinct perspective, such that listeners can follow the line of reasoning.				I & R	M

This table of skills implies that the school district is teaching these skills systematically over the course of a student's K–12 experience. If this is not the case, the teacher will need to review their goals for instruction and students' current abilities. Based upon these two factors, the teacher will need to select the focus for direct instruction in communication skills.

Simply exposing students to rigorous learning opportunities through classroom discussion does little to develop their critical thinking skills (Abrami et al, 2008). Students must be provided with direct instruction in critical analytical thinking and discourse. More specifically, they must be shown how to identify tacit and explicit assumptions, analyze and evaluate the logic of arguments, and create sound arguments of their own. Readers will note that in the aforementioned charts, starting in the fourth grade, students are expected to identify reasons and evidence. This begins with understanding the foundations of argumentation.

Argumentation

In academic discourse, an argument is a group of statements (premises for older students) that lead to a conclusion. Syllogisms, the building blocks for argument creation, are the combination of a general statement (major premise for older students) and a specific statement (minor premise for older students) to reach a conclusion. Syllogisms involve applying deductive reasoning to arrive at a conclusion based on two or more propositions that are asserted or assumed to be true. They are typically written in the following format:

All mammals are animals (major premise).
All elephants are mammals (minor premise).
Therefore, all elephants are animals (conclusion).

Starting in the upper elementary grade levels, students should experience age-appropriate activities requiring them to think backward from a conclusion they express to determine the statements or premises that led to their conclusions. In addition, upper elementary students should have experience creating statements (or premises for older students) that support conclusions.

When it comes to evaluating arguments, there are three important questions students should be taught to use. First, are there different ways to get to the conclusion provided? There are often many possible ways to build to a certain conclusion. Students must learn that some arguments are more effective than others and that some logically valid, true arguments are weak. Second, do the statements logically lead to the conclusion? An argument is valid if the statements lead to the conclusion. A valid argument is not the same as an argument that is agreed upon; it only refers to the structure of the argument. Lastly, is the argument truthful? In an effective argument, all of the premises are statements of truth.

Evidence supporting each statement that is relevant and verifiable is necessary to prove the truth of premises. Students must learn to analyze the following five types of evidence:

- Facts: actual, verifiable, indisputable information. For example, electrons have a negative charge. It is important to remember that facts have a range of reliability. What we know at one point may be subsequently proven false. For example, Pluto was a planet.
- Numbers: statistics, surveys, or any other type of measurement. For the sake of simplicity in teaching and consistency, no matter how certain a number seems, we must insist that students avoid labeling numeric evidence as facts. Students must learn that numbers can be misleading and often fall on a sliding scale of truthfulness. In addition, students must be taught to examine how the numbers were created and that the context of the numbers matters.
- Quotes: the exact words of an expert. To be credible, the credentials of the person being quoted must be legitimate and they must be speaking about their area of expertise. Students must also learn that expertise can be purchased. An expert with no conflict of interest is the most credible.
- Examples: information based on observations. They may be personal anecdotes, items found in text, or experimental results. The source of the evidence is highly relevant as some sources are more credible than others.
- Analogies: comparisons that show how ideas are related or similar to one another. Used effectively, analogies not only support a claim but also clarify it. However, analogies are only valuable if genuine, important similarities between the items exist.

To prove that evidence is effective, students can ask the following three questions: Is there evidence for every statement? Does the evidence match the point of the statement? What is the credibility and quality of the evidence?

The final area of critical thinking students must master for effective participation in academic discussions is identification of common reasoning errors as well as the techniques of persuasion. The following table is a list of errors that are common barriers to quality thought.

Reasoning error	Definition	Example
Generalizing	Taking one incident or example and declaring a global truth from it.	All people in New Jersey go to the beach.
Moving from general to specific	Taking statements that are generally true and applying them incorrectly to a specific situation.	Running is a good way to keep fit, so everyone should run two miles a day.
Derailing the train of thought	Evading the issue by changing the topic.	You bring up gay marriage and claim that I'm against it, but isn't it just as important to talk about the issue of homeless veterans?
Changing the burden of proof	Instead of coming up with proof for their point, the speaker asks their opponent(s) to assume the burden of proof.	No one has proven that ghosts don't exist—can you prove that ghosts don't exist?
Attacking the person	Demeaning the person instead of focusing on the idea.	Even if person A claims _____ it cannot be true because they are an idiot.
Confusing cause and correlation	Assuming that because two things occur simultaneously, one causes the other.	I saw a deer and then I crashed my bike. Deer are bad luck.
Falling for the halo effect	Devaluing or overvaluing the idea of a person because of how impressive they seem.	Isaac Newton believed in alchemy; do you think you know more than Isaac Newton?
Confirmation bias	Noticing only that which confirms what you already think.	Seeking newspaper articles that only support your point of view.
Availability bias	Information that is most readily available or recent dominates our thinking.	Being convinced that flying is unsafe because of a recent plane crash.

It is appropriate to introduce, develop, and reinforce identification of these errors beginning in the fourth grade. By the end of middle school, students should be proficient in identifying these common errors as they are made by speakers during academic discussions.

In order for students to evaluate the message a speaker is attempting to deliver, teachers must teach them common rhetorical tricks used to persuade. Making students aware of these techniques can help them resist rhetoric while remaining focused on the quality of the content of information and ideas.

It is important to emphasize that the use of one of persuasion does not necessarily mean the speaker's core message is invalid. Instead, when using persuasive techniques, the speaker is attempting to influence and manipulate the audience. A simple example is that of a salesman representing a high-quality product using persuasion techniques to get you to buy that product. His use of persuasion techniques does not change the fact that the product is of high quality.

Persuasion technique	Definition	Example
Testimonial	An endorsement by a well-known person.	A famous actor or athlete in a commercial state that they use a certain product.
Plain folks	Referencing ordinary people that the target market can identify with to increase the comfort of an idea.	A commercial shows regular people "just like you" using a product.
Bandwagon	Communicating that everyone else is doing something, so if you want to be accepted and popular, you should do it too.	Nine out of ten people prefer our brand of toothpaste.
Transference	Surrounding the product, person, or idea with things that make people feel good. The hope is that the audience will transfer these positive feelings to the product, person, or idea.	The Presidential Candidate delivers his speech standing in front of several American flags.
Statistics without context	Providing facts or figures that seem to prove the point without any follow-up in the hope that the audience will accept the facts and figures at face value.	Sixty percent of the people on the Earth are malnourished.
Loaded words	Incorporating words known to have a strong emotional impact.	Fascist, Socialist, Communist, tree hugger, liberal, nerd, jock, etc.

Mini-lessons

The most effective vehicle for teaching communication and reasoning skills for academic discussions is the mini-lesson. To avoid overwhelming students, introduce only one skill at a time. Mini-lessons consist of four parts. The first part which introduces the mini-lesson is the connection.

The connection is where you state your teaching point simply, clearly, and explicitly. The purpose is to cue your students so they are ready for the instruction. Your connection must also include an explanation for why you are teaching this idea. The explanation allows the students to understand the importance of the skill or strategy. An example of connection statement for a mini-lesson is: "Today, I am going to teach you how to accurately paraphrase what others say during a discussion, because paraphrasing accurately enables the listener to clarify the speaker's meaning and it conveys interest in what the speaker is saying."

If possible and appropriate, connect the content of your mini-lesson to something you have observed within student discussions. It may be something you noticed with one student or it may be something many students exhibited as a need. An example of this type of statement for an individual is, "In our recent small-group work, I noticed Janet repeat what her partners said in order to clarify her understanding, let me show you all how to do that." An example of this type of statement for identifying a group need is, "I have been listening to your small-group discussions and I noticed that you do not use strategies to clarify your understanding of what the other speakers are saying."

This is not a time for questions and answers. Student talk is limited during a mini-lesson so that the teacher can offer the students direct instruction and then they can practice the new skill or strategy presented.

The next part of the mini-lesson is providing information. When providing information, the language and phrasing used to orient students are important. Use of cues such as "Let me show you what this looks like . . ." or "Let me show you what I mean . . ." signals to the students that they need to get ready for your demonstration.

If appropriate and possible, the demonstration might take the form of showing an example in a video clip. It may also involve a clear explanation of the important points related to the skill, strategy, or behavior. Additionally, information can be provided directly through modeling the skill, strategy, or behavior. When modeling, it is important to explain what you are thinking as you are doing the demonstration. Thinking aloud makes the implicit explicit. Through any combination of these input strategies, students must have a clear understanding of how to use the skill, strategy or behavior in an academic discussion.

During some mini-lessons, it is appropriate to provide students with a few minutes to practice the information taught. During the teaching demonstration, the new skill or strategy was modeled. This time provides an opportunity for students to get guided, hands-on practice, in preparation for their independent application of the strategy later. This guided practice time also offers the teacher the opportunity to assess student understanding and application of the information. If it appears students are confused or are not correctly applying the information provided, then reteaching should occur. If it is not appropriate to provide students with practice time, then at a minimum, they should be provided with the opportunity to share what they noticed during the demonstration.

The final part of the mini-lesson requires the teacher to reiterate the key points and link this information to what students will be doing during the upcoming discussion. It is appropriate at this point to direct students to set a personal goal for using the skill and to let them know they will be asked to self-assess their performance at the conclusion of the discussion.

Making these skills public through a wall chart is a valuable strategy for reinforcing skills over time. The following is a completed template that can be used to plan a mini-lesson for academic discussions. A blank copy of this template can be found in the appendix.

Mini-lesson planning template	
Grade level: 5th	Subject: Science
Topic: Energy	
CONNECT: Students learn why today's instruction is important to them as discussion participants and how the lesson relates to their prior work. The topic of instruction is stated here.	Today I am going to be teaching you how to link your comments to those made by others. In our discussion past week, I noticed that someone would present an idea and instead of considering that idea and building upon it, we switched to other ideas. Because we did not link our ideas to those of other class members, our discussion stayed at the surface level, and we did not expand our thinking about the topic.
TEACH: The teacher gives information about the skill. This information may be provided by giving an explanation, showing examples, or through demonstration.	I am going to role-play a conversation with Adam. In this role-play, I am going to link my comments to the ideas he expresses. As you watch, please take notes on what you see me do and what I say. Role-Play (Activity) Now that you have observed the use of this skill, let's record on the chart paper the things that you saw me do and what you heard me say. Record student responses—add to them if necessary.

(Continued)

(Continued)

Grade level: 5th	Subject: Science
Topic: Energy	
HAVE-A-GO: After teaching the skill, students are given a chance to quickly practice what has been taught or to share what they noticed about the demonstration.	Please turn to your elbow partner and have a quick talk about their favorite TV show. In the conversation you have, build upon the initial ideas by using the linking strategies we have just identified.
LINK: The teacher reiterates what has been taught. Students are reminded how this lesson relates to their work in discussions, setting a goal for the use of the skill.	Today in our discussion, our goal is to link our comments to those of the person speaking. At the end of the discussion, you will be asked to reflect on how well you used this strategy and how well we used it as a class.

SELF-RATING OF STUDENT PREPARATION FOR DISCUSSIONS

How do I provide students with the content knowledge, communication, and reasoning skills required to participate effectively in discussions?					
The teacher provides appropriate student preparation activities and systematically teaches essential communication and reasoning skills.					
Teacher Evidence: • The teacher assigns students activities in advance that are designed to prepare them for the discussion. • The teacher has selected content for mini-lessons based on identified student needs or district curriculum documents. • The teacher follows the four-part model for delivery of mini-lessons.		**Student Evidence:** • Students come to the discussion with evidence of having prepared in advance. • When asked, students can explain the content and purpose of the teacher mini-lesson.			
	Innovating (4.0)	*Applying (3.0)*	*Developing (2.0)*	*Beginning (1.0)*
Student Preparation	My use of this standard is creative enough to be shared with other faculty members so they can use it with their students.	I prepare my students with the content knowledge, communication and reasoning skills they need to participate in discussions.	I attempt to prepare my students with the content knowledge, communication, and reasoning skills required for discussion participation but the results of my attempts are frequently ineffective.	I have made minimal effort to prepare my students with the content knowledge, communication, and reasoning skills required for participation in discussions.

TEACHER'S ROLE IN THE DISCUSSION

With preparation for the discussion completed, attention shifts to the teacher's role in initiating, sustaining, closing, and possibly extending thinking about the content of the discussion. Initiating the discussion involves reviewing the norms, teaching the mini-lesson on communication or reasoning, activating student thinking, and presenting the focus question.

Initiating the discussion

Reviewing the norms with students and teaching a specific skill provides focus for the behavior expected for the discussion. Once this has been completed, it is time to activate student thinking on the discussion topic. A pre-discussion warm-up on the content for the discussion facilitates student focus on the topic and encourages students to generate ideas. There are many options for a warm-up activity. The following are examples of activities that can be used for this purpose.

Brainstorm and Categorize

Directions:

1. Form pairs of students.
2. Present the topic to students and have them brainstorm what they know about topic. Specify the time limit for brainstorming.
3. When time has expired, have students sort their ideas into category groups.
4. Have students label the categories.
5. Students can place their information on chart paper. These charts can be hung and revisited after the discussion.

Five Words—Three Words

Directions:

1. Have students individually list five words that come to mind when they think of the topic for discussion.
2. Pair students to have them share and discuss their words.
3. Direct each pair to select any three of those words.
4. Select a few random pairs to share and explain their words to the entire class.

Paired Verbal Fluency

Directions:

1. Place students into pairs and have them identify as number 1 or 2 in each pair.
2. Announce the topic.

3. Provide student 1 with forty-five seconds to share everything he or she knows about the topic. During this time, student 2 is only listening.
4. Switch roles with student 2 now adding more information.
5. Complete another round of sharing with 30 seconds of sharing time.
6. Ask students to record ideas they want to ask about or clarify and questions they have about the topic.

Synectics

Directions:

1. Elicit from students or provide the name of a familiar everyday object.
2. Pose the question "What are the ways _____ (the discussion topic) is like _____ (the familiar object)." For example: "What are all the ways an atom is like a grapefruit?"
3. In pairs, have students generate as many connections as they can within the time frame allotted.
4. Select random pairs of students to share their connections.

Write-Pair-Share

Directions:

1. Provide a prompt related to the discussion topic.
2. Provide students with time to write a response.
3. Form pairs: label one partner as 1 and the other as 2.
4. Prove student 1 with a timed opportunity to share his or her response while student 2 listens.
5. Switch roles.
6. Randomly select a few students to share what their respective partner said with the rest of the class.

With student knowledge activated, it is now time to pose the initial focus question. It is important to present the question in a way that demonstrates you care about student responses. The facial and vocal expression as well as the words used must convey sincere interest in student ideas as well as enthusiasm for the topic. In addition, as you present the question, attempt to make eye contact with each student. This will signal you are interested in everyone's ideas.

SELF-RATING OF INITIATING TEACHER-LED CLASSROOM DISCUSSIONS

How do I initiate classroom discussions?				
The teacher uses strategies to activate student thinking related to the discussion topic and presents the focus question.				
Teacher Evidence: • The teacher uses an activity intended to focus student thinking and idea generation related to the discussion topic. • The teacher presents the focus question in a manner that demonstrates enthusiasm for the topic and interest in student responses.		**Student Evidence:** • Student behavior demonstrates focus on the topic for discussion. • The classroom discussion begins with student-generated responses. • When asked, students indicate that the teacher is genuinely interested in their thoughts related to the topic of discussion.		
	Innovating (4.0)	*Applying (3.0)*	*Developing (2.0)*	*Beginning (1.0)*
Initiating Classroom Discussions	My use of this standard is creative enough to be shared with other faculty members so they can use it with their students.	I use explicit strategies to initiate classroom discussions. My strategies activate student thinking on the discussion topic. In addition, my introduction of the focus question demonstrates my enthusiasm for the topic and interest in student responses.	I attempt to initiate classroom discussions, but the results of my attempts are frequently ineffective.	I have made minimal effort to initiate classroom discussions.

Sustaining the discussion

Once the discussion has started, the teacher has two primary roles. First, the teacher becomes a facilitator of student thinking. Second, the teacher must strive to ensure there is equitable student participation.

Think-time

In classrooms, there are pressures and demands on teachers' time. Pacing guides and high stakes testing can make it very difficult to provide students with the time they require to think deeply. Perhaps this is the reason teachers typically do not provide sufficient wait-time after asking a question or receiving an answer.

Research findings on the effects of providing three to five seconds both after asking a question (Think-Time 1) and after hearing an answer (Think-Time 2) are consistently positive. When teachers provide these think times, more students participate in class discussions, their answers are longer and of higher quality, and achievement improves on cognitively complex measures (Walsh & Sattes, 2005). Unfortunately, research also indicates that teachers rarely pause after asking questions and getting responses. According to Cotton (1988), the average wait-time teachers allow after posing a question is one second or less.

We cannot have it both ways when it comes to the quality of thinking and speed. In conducting academic discussions in which we seek to give students a chance to expand their ideas, we cannot rush to cover curriculum. Because quality of thinking and speed are anathema to each other, we must choose which goal is more important.

Unfortunately, traditional school practices have trained students to cut their thinking short. Because class time is limited, students provide minimal answers. Requiring students to work together to expand, connect, and elaborate on what they are learning is a major shift in how we are expecting students to learn.

Expecting students to honor think times before answering a question and after hearing a response is not a normal practice in most classrooms. Teachers need to create a culture that honors this silence so that everyone has a chance to listen to and understand what has been said. This can be accomplished in teacher-guided discussions by explaining the purpose of think-times to students, modeling the behavior explicitly, and prompting students to allow time for thought.

Probing student responses

It would be reasonable to expect that if a teacher were to ask a higher-level question, he or she would get a student response at that same level of thought. It turns out that this assumption related to questioning is incorrect. Nearly half of student answers are at a different cognitive level than the teacher's question (Walsh & Sattes, 2005). Yet, teachers generally accept these answers without probing or prompting correct responses.

Probes are statements or questions designed to prompt student thinking. Probing student responses can occur following either a correct or incorrect response. With regard to the timing of probes, extended teacher statements should only occur after a significant pause in the exchange of ideas. It is important to avoid unnecessarily interrupting students during a discussion.

Probes are not judgments of student responses. Students who fear being judged or penalized will rarely if ever participate in academic discussions. Students who receive praise for their answers get the message that the teacher is looking for correct answers. Thus, when we evaluate student responses, either positively or negatively, we are working against a climate in which new and innovative ideas flourish.

To extend individual thinking and speaking, it is better to make a short statement of interest in what the student is saying. For example, "Tony you seem to have a different view on this issue, please tell us more about what you are thinking." Another option is to encourage a student to keep speaking with statements such as "Please continue" or "Tell us more." Yet another way to extend student thinking is to paraphrase the response and offer a personal reflection. For example, "I think I heard you say that school uniforms would be against students' first amendment rights. I had not thought about it that way. I am interested in hearing more about the reasons you believe that is true."

Sometimes a question is an appropriate means for extending student thinking. When a question incorporates a part of a student's idea or previous response and is followed by a request for further elaboration, it can increase student thinking and engagement (Walsh & Sattes, 2015). For example, "Jennifer you stated that a universal minimum wage would be bad for our economy. Can you say more about why you think this would be a bad idea?" The critical feature of this type of question is that it keeps the responsibility for thinking with the student.

Clarifying and correcting

Students may have an idea, but they experience difficulty expressing it clearly. If understanding is elusive, the teacher can respond productively by assuming responsibility for the lack of understanding. For example, "Can you explain that again? I am not sure that I understood you." Phrased in this manner, the question does not place responsibility for confusion on the student, but it simply provides them with another opportunity to help the teacher understand.

When a student makes a statement containing a factual error, the teacher can respond with a declarative statement that draws attention to that error. For example, in response to the student statement, "Obesity is caused by people eating too much and being lazy," the teacher can make the statement, "From our reading we learned that it is true that lifestyle choices may contribute to obesity, but it also can be a genetic disorder." A statement such as this encourages the student to both continue the discussion and strive for accuracy when making statements.

Encouraging connections

An academic discussion goal is the building of ideas. In order to build ideas, discussion participants need to connect to and build upon the ideas of others. Students must understand that academic discussions are cooperative, not competitive, endeavors.

A teacher can model the concept of linking ideas by connecting what one student says to the idea of a previous student. For example, "Sam, your idea about reducing carbon emissions connects to what Dan said earlier." Another strategy is to use a student's insight to maintain an important content thread followed by inviting other students to build on this insight. For example, "Tommy said about 44 million Americans owe more than 1.5 trillion in student debt. I wonder what this says about the value of a college education in America today." Lastly, the teacher can invite students to formulate and pose questions. For example, "Ellen has said that social media enables the spread of unreliable and false information. I am wondering if Ellen's comments raise any questions or concerns from anyone else about social media."

Troubleshooting. There are two potentially troublesome issues a teacher may confront when guiding a classroom discussion. First, students may purposefully or unwittingly stray from the topic of discussion. While it is desirable to encourage creative thinking, we need to make sure that discussions promote the intended academic outcomes. Students need to learn to discipline their thinking in pursuit of shared understanding. When this happens, the teacher could pose a question such as, "Carlos, how does your comment connect with today's discussion topic?" You might also use a statement that acknowledges the student's comment while redirecting the conversation focus. For example, "Kesha, your comment is intriguing but it does not seem relevant to today's discussion topic. Write it in your notebook so that we can revisit it if we discuss that issue."

A worry that many teachers have when they first begin to use guided classroom discussions is that students will talk very little. Initially, this may be true. Students are not used to teachers demonstrating genuine interest in what they are thinking. It may take time and patience for students to come to the realization that you are asking them expand and go further with their own thinking.

It is also true that sometimes discussions lose steam. When this happens, providing silent think-time is often enough for students to gather their thoughts and generate new ideas. Another possibility is to pose a new, related focus question. Having prepared follow-up questions that you can use is a good strategy for dealing with discussions that do not produce the quantity or quality of conversation desired.

Additionally, you could provide students with a few minutes to record their thoughts and/or develop a question they have about the conversation topic up to this point. If appropriately related to the topic, student-generated questions could serve as the springboard for continued discussion.

Ensuring equitable participation. Too often classroom discussions involve only the most confident students. As a result, we ignore what is happening in the minds of those students that do not volunteer to participate. This is particularly true for students perceived as slow or poor learners (Cotton, 1988). An effective teacher does not leave student participation to chance.

One of the strategies a teacher can use to encourage all students to participate has already been explained. When students feel connected to their teacher on a personal level and the classroom norms support a climate encouraging the sharing of ideas, all students are more likely to participate in discussions.

Other strategies a teacher may use to encourage participation is to be intentional in moving around the classroom. Standing in a different position every few minutes encourages students who are in your proximity to attend to the discussion. Making eye contact with a pleasant facial expression is another nonverbal behavior that will cue students of your desire for them to share their thoughts. If all else fail, it is sometimes necessary to use the traditional mode of questioning. Occasionally, you may need to call on an individual student to respond. However, this must remain the exception and not the rule.

One strategy to avoid when attempting to get all students to participate is awarding points to those that make contributions. This teacher action sends the wrong message about the value of discussion. The message sent by the teacher awarding points is that you need to comply with this activity or I will not reward you. In this scenario, grade-conscious students will attempt to dominate the discussion while other students will make the minimum contributions necessary to earn the points. Once these students have made their "required" number of contributions they will no longer participate. Students who do not care about grades will likely choose not to participate at all.

True academic discussion requires commitment. It is hard work to do the type of thinking required for genuine academic discourse. If students are to put forth the effort required, they will need to have the commitment that is characteristic of intrinsic motivation. They must come to value academic discussions as a means for exploring and building their ideas, not as an opportunity for earning participation points.

SELF-RATING OF SUSTAINING CLASSROOM DISCUSSIONS

How do I facilitate student thinking and ensure equitable participation in the discussion?			
The teacher uses strategies to facilitate student thinking and ensure that student participation in the discussion is equitable.			
Teacher Evidence: • An appropriate amount of wait-time is provided before and after answering questions. • Non-evaluative probes are used to extend student thinking. • Clarifying and correcting is done in a manner that encourages continued discussion and accuracy when making statements. • Teacher behavior encourages the linking of student ideas. • Teacher behavior encourages all students to participate in the discussion.				**Student Evidence:** • Students wait before and after they answer a question. • When asked, students understand the reason for providing wait-time. • Students link their ideas to the ideas of others. • All students participate in the discussion.
	Innovating (4.0)	Applying (3.0)	Developing (2.0)	Beginning (1.0)
Sustaining Discussions	My use of this standard is creative enough to be shared with other faculty members so they can use it with their students.	I use explicit strategies that facilitate student thinking and all of the students participate in classroom discussions.	I attempt to facilitate student thinking and ensure equitable student participation, but the results of my attempts are frequently ineffective.	I have made minimal effort to facilitate student thinking and ensure equitable participation in classroom discussions.

Facilitating discussion closure

Consensus is not the goal for a classroom discussion. We do not seek to have students agree with one another or the teacher. Instead, we seek for each student to reach a larger and more sophisticated understanding of ideas.

Content closure

In the sequence of classroom discussions, the goal for closure is to provide students with the opportunity to reflect on the content. Students need this opportunity to summarize their understanding of the content discussed.

Additionally, students need an opportunity to reflect on individual and collective performance of discussion skills. The following are varied structures individual students can use to reflect on content.

Geometric close

Directions:

1. Draw a triangle, square, and circle horizontally on the board or a piece of chart paper.
2. Direct students to record the following:
    a. Something in the discussion that "squared" with what they already thought. (Square)
    b. Something they see from a new angle as a result of the discussion. (Triangle)
    c. A remaining question that is still circling around in their mind. (Circle)

3*2*1

Directions:

1. Direct students to write down:
    a. Three things they learned about the topic from the discussion.
    b. Two questions or things that continue to puzzle them about this topic.
    c. One idea for how they might answer their question or explore the puzzles remaining.

Ticket to leave

Directions:

1. On a slip of paper have students write one important thing they learned from the discussion and one question that has left them puzzled.
2. Students hand their "ticket" to the teacher as they leave class.
3. If there is time, random students can be selected to share their tickets with the rest of the class.

Draw a picture or diagram

Directions:

1. Provide students with a piece of blank paper.
2. Have students either create a symbol or sketch an image that best captures the main ideas of the discussion.

3. If there is time, students can be placed in pairs to explain their images.

Learning log

Directions:

1. If students already are keeping a learning log, then direct students to write a new entry. If not, provide students with a sheet of paper.
2. Direct students to record a response to a teacher-created prompt. The prompt can be specific to the content or it can be more general. A prompt that works particularly well for discussions is the following: I used to think _____ but now after our discussion I think_____.

Process reflection

Reflection on the individual's performance as well as the group's collective performance is essential for continued development of communication and reasoning skills. We do not learn as much from our experiences as we do from reflecting upon them. The ideal time for this reflection on performance is immediately following the discussion. The adaptable prompts given next can be used to prompt student reflection on individual and group discussion skills:

- What did you do well in our discussion today?
- What part of the discussion process was difficult for you?
- What goal can you set for our next discussion?
- What could you have done differently to improve this discussion?
- How effectively did you use the skill presented in today's mini-lesson?

These prompts can be answered separately or recorded as part of the assignment provided for content closure. Another option is to provide or have students create a three-column table. In the first column, students record the focus from the mini-lesson. In the second column, students use a continuum to rate their individual performance. Underneath the continuum, they provide support for their self-rating. The third column is the same format as the second column except the focus is on collective performance. The figure given next is a complete example of this format.

Directions: In column 1, record the skill that was the focus of today's mini-lesson. Next rate your use of this skill in today's discussion as VG (very good), OK, or NI (needs improvement). In the space below, provide an explanation for your rating. Next, do the same thing for the class performance. Finally, in the bottom box, identify how you think we can improve our future discussions.

Mini-lesson focus	Individual performance	Class performance
Asking questions to clarify the speaker's message.	VG ---(ok)----- NI I asked one question because I did not understand. I could have asked more but I focused too much on trying to prove my own point.	VG ---(ok)----- NI A couple of people were really good at asking clarifying questions. Sometimes it seemed forced instead of natural.
To improve our future discussions, we should review this skill. We should discuss when to use it so it does not make our discussion awkward and slow.		

The written student reflections should be collected and reviewed by the teacher. This information serves as valuable formative feedback that can be used for planning future mini-lesson topics. Combined with the teacher's own observations, the student feedback may lead to the decision to teach a new skill or perhaps reteach the skill that was the focus for that lesson.

Depending upon the time available, a teacher may decide to engage in a whole-class discussion on the group's performance as a follow-up activity to the written reflection. Because the focus of the whole-class discussion should be on the group's performance, the teacher will still need to collect student responses to review individual performance ratings.

SELF-RATING OF CLASSROOM DISCUSSION CLOSURE

How do I provide opportunities for reflection on the content of and process used for discussions?	
The teacher uses strategies to provide students with the opportunity to reflect on the content of and processes used for classroom discussions.	
Teacher Evidence: • Structured opportunities are provided for students to reflect on the content of the discussion. • Structured opportunities are provided for students to reflect on both the individual and collective use of discussion skills. • The teacher collects the products of reflection and reviews them as part of planning for future teacher-led discussions.	**Student Evidence:** • Student responses demonstrate a more comprehensive, sophisticated understanding of the discussion topic. • Student responses demonstrate an honest appraisal of both individual and class use of communication and reasoning skills.

(Continued)

(Continued)

	Innovating (4.0)	Applying (3.0)	Developing (2.0)	Beginning (1.0)
Discussion Closure	My use of this standard is creative enough to be shared with other faculty members so they can use it with their students.	I use explicit strategies to provide students with the opportunity to reflect on the content of and processes used for classroom discussions.	I attempt to use strategies to provide students with the opportunity to reflect on the content of and processes used for classroom discussions, but the results of my attempts are frequently ineffective.	I have made minimal effort to provide opportunities for reflection on the content of and processes used for classroom discussions.

Student assessment

Unfortunately, in some school districts, anything that takes significant instructional time either should or must have an academic grade attached to it. Whereas descriptive feedback provided to students and self-assessment can promote improved performance, the possibility of receiving a number or letter grade for individual classroom discussions can have a negative impact. In addition, unless the discussion is recorded and watched repeatedly, it would be impossible to validly measure student performance. A teacher cannot focus on modeling discussion skills and scaffolding student thinking at the same time they are collecting data on student performance.

Rubrics for academic discussions can be found at https://www.teacherspayteachers.com/Store/The-Assessment-Guy. The rubrics on this site rubrics align to the discussion skills presented earlier in this chapter. While these rubrics can be used to provide a numeric score for individual student performance, they are more valuable as a formative assessment tool. On a regular basis, such as at the mid-point of a marking period, students can receive a completed copy of this rubric and use it to set goals for improving their individual performance.

If an individual grade must be assigned, then it is more appropriate to have students complete a follow-up assignment to the discussion. Writing assignments completed after discussions help students further consolidate their thinking and often have content that is superior to writing assignments without the benefit of prior discussion. Prompts should require students to provide evidence from the text and/or classroom discussion. For example:

- In our pre-reading and today's discussion, we discussed whether the United States should implement a carbon cap and trade system. In your essay, take a pro or con stance on this issue. *Use evidence from our discussion and the required readings to support your position.*

A rubric like the one that follows could be used to evaluate and, if necessary, grade student responses.

Response rubric				
	Score 3.0	Score 2.0	Score 1.0	Score 0
RESPONSE TO PROMPT	Response addresses all of the required parts of the prompt.	Response addresses most of the required parts of the prompt.	Response addresses some parts of the prompt.	Response does not address the requirements of the prompt.
COMPREHENSION	Response demonstrates thorough understanding of the topic.	Response demonstrates adequate understanding of the topic.	Response demonstrates partial understanding of the topic.	Response does not demonstrate understanding of the topic.
EVIDENCE	It provides relevant, detailed support from the text and discussion.	It provides adequate support from text and discussion.	Evidence provided is inadequate.	No evidence is provided.

SELF-RATING SUMMARY AND PERSONAL GOAL SETTING FOR GROWTH

Directions: Transfer your scores from each of the previous rating scales to the following table. Based on your personal profile, select a goal for improving in teacher-led classroom discussions. Make your goal specific, measurable, realistic, and time-bound. For example, *I will achieve the applying level of sustaining teacher-led discussions by the date of my annual summative review.* Next, describe the specific action steps you will take to reach this goal and evidence you will use to demonstrate goal attainment.

Teacher-led discussion profile				
Teacher-led discussion domain	Rating			
	Innovating	*Applying*	*Developing*	*Beginning*
Classroom discussion environment				
Focus question development				
Student preparation				
Initiating discussions				
Sustaining discussions				
Discussion closure				
Based on my profile, my goal is to:				
To achieve this goal, I will:				
I know that I will have achieved this goal when:				

This chapter has provided a five-step process for teacher-guided discussions. From planning for the discussion to facilitating to closure, this chapter has provided the information necessary for a teacher to conduct disciplined academic discussions in order to promote deep thinking. This process is similar to the steps that are used to implement structured small-group academic discussions. The similarities as well as critical differences are the subject of chapter 2.

Chapter 3

Structured Small-Group Discussions

Teacher-guided discussions are the most appropriate vehicle when students are first learning the norms and skills for effective discussions. However, once students understand discussion norms and have developed a basic level of communication and reasoning skills, when appropriate, the teacher must begin to introduce small-group discussion activities. Small-group discussions are defined as protocols in which two to five students are tied together by the common purpose to complete a discussion task and include every group member.

Small-group discussions are superior to teacher-guided discussions in one important way. When done correctly, small-group discussions increase the quantity of opportunities for students to speak. Instead of one person speaking at a time as is the case in teacher-guided discussions, multiple students are talking simultaneously during small-group discussions. This increases opportunities for making meaning related to the topic. Of course, to achieve this benefit, we must ensure that this participation is not dominated by individual group members. The content presented later in this chapter is designed to ensure equitable participation by students.

A second reason for implementing small-group discussions is that social interactions and teamwork are increasingly necessary skills for success in the work place (Conley, 2014). Employers are frequently requiring employees to function in teams to complete tasks and solve complex problems. Therefore, students who are skilled and experienced with small-group discussions will be more prepared for success in the work force of the future.

Considering these two reasons for small-group discussions, it is incumbent upon teachers to create a balance between teacher-guided and small-group discussions. Depending upon the purpose of the discussion and the nature of the topic, there are times when teacher-guided discussions will remain the most appropriate strategy. This is especially true when it is early in the learning process. Later in the learning process, small-group discussions are potentially more effective.

Despite the advantages, it is important to recognize that structured small-group discussions can be challenging to implement. Whereas it may be easy to get the students to socialize, it can be difficult to get them to learn socially. This type of learning requires specific skills and techniques students must learn and develop.

This chapter and the next will address two types of small-group discussions. The focus for this chapter will be on implementing highly structured small-group discussion protocols. These protocols scaffold many of the communication skills required for effective discussions. While the discussion involves many students at one time, the teacher controls the process.

Structured small-group discussion protocols are most appropriate as a part of a larger lesson. They are highly effective means of activating prior knowledge, facilitating rehearsal of new information and enabling students to summarize what they have learned. Because of the amount of structure, the intended purpose and the time required, use of these protocols does not require most of the steps in the five-step cycle described for teacher-guided discussions. However, use of these protocols does require the teacher to select the one that will best meet the intended instructional purpose.

STRUCTURED SMALL-GROUP DISCUSSION PROTOCOLS

Each of the following protocols requires students to complete multiple steps. To ensure that directions are clear and that students are able to follow them, consider using the following two suggestions. First, give one direction at a time, having students complete that step before receiving the next step in the directions. This is especially important the first few times you use the protocol. Second, if possible, post the directions during work time so students can refer to them as necessary.

While completing the activities in these protocols, students will create productive noise. Thus, it is necessary for the teacher to have a strategy for gaining student attention. Instead of raising voice levels to get students' attention, a teacher can train students to respond to the "quiet signal." This simple procedure requires the teacher to raise his or her hand. When student's see this raised hand, they are to stop talking and doing followed by raising their own hand. While having their hand raised, students are to look at the teacher and listen for the information that will follow.

The following are eleven protocols a teacher can select from to conduct structured small-group discussions.

Present-pause

Purpose: Present-pause is an excellent strategy for increasing comprehension of lectures, audio-visual presentations, and reading informational text. As it requires minimal advance planning and only minor changes to typical instructional practices, it is one of the easiest protocols to implement.

Directions:

1. Arrange students into pairs or trios.
2. Present content for approximately five minutes (or have students read a section of text). Students are to take notes (or annotate text) during this time period.
3. Pause for approximately two minutes. During the pause, pairs or trios share their notes, filling in gaps in their own notes and assisting one another in clarifying concepts. During this time students are not allowed to ask the teacher a question. This helps build interdependence among students, forcing them to rely on one another for help.
4. Repeat the cycle until all of the content has been presented or the section of text has been read.
5. Provide several minutes at the end of the presentation or reading to allow students to ask the teacher unresolved questions or issues.

Choices

Purpose: This structured small-group discussion activity is valuable for sharing information with others that have the same viewpoint on a given topic.

Directions:

1. Choose three, four, or five alternatives and post them in the corners of the room.
2. Introduce the choices to the students.
3. Provide students with an appropriate amount of think-time and have them record their choice.
4. Have students move to and then stand by their choice. If only one student moves to a choice, validate his or her selection but then ask him or her to move to his or her second option.
5. Direct students to form, or assign students to pairs.

6. Have each person in the pair identify as 1 or 2.
7. Provide person 1 with an appropriate amount of time to share the reasons for his or her choice. Person 2 is listening, but may offer comments designed to clarify and extend person 1's thinking. They may not offer information intended to support their reasons until it is their turn.
8. Switch roles.
9. Randomly select several students to share the main points of their discussion with the rest of the class.

People Graph

Purpose: Similar to choices, people graphs provide students with the opportunity to share information with those that have a similar viewpoint on a topic.

Directions:

1. Form a Likert scale on the floor by evenly spacing out five sheets of paper. Label the papers as: SA (Strongly Agree), A (Agree), N (Neutral), D (Disagree), and SD (Strongly Disagree).
2. Present students with a statement that creates a continuum of opinions.
3. Provide adequate think time and then have students record their choice.
4. On the teacher's signal, students go to the spot on the scale that represents their selection.
5. Direct students to form, or assign students to pairs.
6. Have each person in the pair identify as 1 or 2.
7. Provide 1 with an appropriate amount of time to share the reasons for his or her choice. Person 2 is listening but may offer comments designed to clarify and extend person 1's thinking. They may not offer reasons to support their own point of view until it is their turn.
8. Switch roles.
9. Randomly select several students to share the main points of their discussion with the rest of the class.

Concentric Circles

Purpose: Concentric circles is a more flexible small-group discussion structure than choices or people graphs. It allows for a wide range of questions because it does not require a forced choice. Any question that could be asked to the whole group is suitable for this discussion structure.

Directions:

1. Form students into one large circle.
2. Going around the circle, have students label themselves as a 1 or 2.

3. Direct all students with the 1 label to take a giant step forward. Next, have them turn toward the members of the outside circle and slide to the right to make sure they are in front of a 2. You should know have two concentric circles consisting of student pairs. If you have an extra person, you can pair two students in the outside circle to form a group of three.
4. The teacher asks a question and then provides an appropriate amount of think-time for students to formulate a response.
5. Direct students in the inside circle to share their responses. The outside circle is only listening, but may offer comments designed to clarify and extend their partners thinking. They may not offer their own thoughts until is their turn.
6. Switch roles.
7. Randomly select several students to share the main points of their discussion with the rest of the class.
8. Have students in the inside-circle rotate one person clockwise and repeat the process with either the same question or a different one.

Three-step Interview

Purpose: The Three-step Interview can be used as an entrance activity to introduce the topic and to activate prior knowledge; as an in-between activity to encourage students to analyze and understand the topic in depth; and as an exit task to review the information taught in the class.

Directions:

1. Have students form or assign students to pairs.
2. Label each student as 1 or 2.
3. Provide students with a general content related topic.
4. Provide all students with an appropriate amount of think-time.
5. Direct student 1 to interview person 2 about the topic. Person 1 may take notes while person 2 is speaking.
6. After providing a predetermined amount of interview time, have students switch roles.
7. After both partners have been interviewed, pair each team with another pair to form a group of four.
8. In groups of four, each person is provided with time to share what their partner said during the interview.

Consensus Statements

Purpose: Consensus Statements are a valuable structured small-group discussion activity for facilitating students' synthesis of ideas.

Directions:

1. Have students form or assign pairs.
2. Provide a starter prompt. For example, recycling is important because . . .
3. Provide time for students to individually write a response.
4. In turn, have each student share his or statement with their partner. There is no discussion of statements until each partner has shared their response.
5. Direct pairs to discuss the individual statements to determine what they share in common and what is different.
6. Direct pairs to create one statement capturing the most important parts of what each partner expressed in their individual statement. It is important to instruct and perhaps demonstrate for students how to do this step. The goal is not the creation of one-long run-on sentence.
7. Randomly select several pairs to share their consensus statement. They can also be posted for all to view.

Rotating Responses

Purpose: This is an excellent strategy for generating ideas. It can also be extended to include categorizing information.

Directions:

1. Post one piece of chart paper per prompt. Spread the paper evenly throughout the outside of the room. Write the question or prompt on the chart (or next to it if you will be using this strategy for multiple classes in a day).
2. Assign or have students form evenly distributed groups at each chart. For example, if you have five charts and twenty-five students, then it will be five students per chart.
3. Have each group select the first recorder and distribute a different colored marker to each group.
4. Provide the following directions to students. "Write response to the question/topic. You will have ____ (time). When I make my signal to stop, please finish the response you are currently writing."
5. After the specified time, give the signal to stop recording. Direct the recorder to hand the marker to a different person in the group (should be someone that has not recorded responses yet). Have each group rotate one chart clockwise.
6. Upon arriving at the next chart, direct students to mark ideas they agree with using a plus sign and place a question mark next to ideas they are not sure about.

7. Upon your signal, students repeat the process of adding new information (no repeats) to the chart. Repeat this process until students are back to their original chart.
8. An option is to have students review the ideas at their original chart, organizing them into categories.
9. Another option is to have students do a timed rotation to each chart in order to review all of the information recorded (and categorized if that has been completed).
10. Have students return to their seats and if appropriate, as a large group review information recorded on the charts, especially question marks. Having different colors for each group will help you identify which group wrote the original statement and which group has the question.

The Last Word

Purpose: This strategy is an excellent format for small-group discussion of text.

Directions:

1. Require students to read and annotate a text.
2. Assign or have students form groups of four.
   a. If you have one extra student, form groups of four and one group of five.
   b. If you have two extra students, form two groups of three and make the rest groups of four.
   c. If you have three extra students, form one group of three with the rest groups of four.
3. Identify the first speaker in the group.
4. Provide the speaker with two minutes of uninterrupted time to introduce an important idea from the text. He or she must identify the location of the information in the text, and either:
   a. explain why the idea is important,
   b. agree or disagree with the author, or
   c. pose a question related to the author's idea.
5. In turn, every other group member has a maximum of one minute to comment on the speaker's statement by:
   a. adding to it,
   b. clarifying, or
   c. presenting a different point of view.

6. After all group members have had their turn to speak, the initial speaker is given one minute to provide the last word. This is the opportunity for him or her to clarify their thinking about the idea introduced.

Text-analysis

Purpose: This is an excellent strategy for analyzing text at the sentence, phrase, and word levels.

Directions:

1. Direct students to read a common text and identify the following:
   a. A sentence that is important to the overall meaning of the passage.
   b. A phrase that moved, engaged, provoked, or was in some other way personally meaningful.
   c. A word that was especially powerful.
2. Have students form or assign students to groups of four (for odd numbers see step 2 in the Last Word).
3. Identify person 1 in each group. Starting with that person and going clockwise, each person will share his or her selected sentence. They are to point to the location of the sentence in the passage and explain why that specific sentence was chosen. Each student is provided with one minute to complete this step. Other group members may ask clarifying questions or prompt the student to extend their thinking, but they may not offer their own ideas at this time.
4. After each group member has shared their selected sentence, they are to conduct a discussion of the commonalities in these sentences. Two minutes are provided for the group to reach consensus regarding the sentence that best embodies the overall meaning of the text. This selected sentence is recorded on a piece of paper for later sharing with the whole class.
5. This process is repeated for the phrase and then the word.
6. Whole class sharing of responses occurs when each group is finished.

Verbal Tug of War

Purpose: Verbal tug of war is an excellent strategy for building student's persuasion skills through discussion of a controversial issue.

Directions:

1. Select a topic for which there are two clearly divided opinions. Develop a "yes/no" proposition. For example, should schools have a dress code?

2. Provide students with think time and have them record their choice.
3. Direct students to stand on the side of the room that represents their choice. They must choose one side or the other.
4. Select one speaker from either side to speak first. The speaker's objective is to persuade the students on the other side to change their initial position. When the speaker has finished, those who have been persuaded to change their position silently switch to that side. Not allowing applause or comments encourages civility.
5. Repeat the process by selecting someone from the other side to speak.
6. Continue selecting speakers until either everyone has had a turn or until discussion of the issue has been exhausted.

Fishbowl Discussion

Purpose: This strategy is excellent for discussion of a common reading or an unresolved or controversial issue.

Directions:

1. Have students read and annotate a common text.
2. Create two circles in the classroom. The inside circle will have five chairs facing one another. The outside circle will seat the remaining students and will be facing the inside circle.
3. Assign five students to be in the "fishbowl" to start the discussion.
4. State the rule that only students in the "fishbowl" are allowed to speak during the activity.
5. The outside circle of students are responsible for providing "food for thought" (strip of paper or sticky note) with relevant information that can be passed to an inside circle participant. In addition, they are expected to take notes during the discussion. These notes can focus on the content of the discussion, the process of the discussion, or both.
6. Once a student in the circle has spoken twice, a student from the outside circle may tap that student on the shoulder and switch places. After speaking four times, the student on the inside must tap out by selecting a person in the outer circle. This process continues for the length of the discussion.
7. In a large class, it is possible to have two separate groups occurring simultaneously.
8. If desired, the teacher can have two to four separate discussion questions. After completing the first question, the teacher can begin the next question by changing the composition of the original groups.

SELF-RATING OF IMPLEMENTATION OF STRUCTURED SMALL-GROUP DISCUSSION PROTOCOLS

How do I use structured small-group discussion protocols to meet instructional objectives?	
The teacher implements structured small-group discussion protocols to meet intended instructional objectives.	
Teacher Evidence: • The teacher selects protocols appropriate for the intended purpose. • The teacher systematically provides students with directions for completing the protocol. • Directions for completing the protocol are posted. • The teacher correctly implements the steps of the protocol. • The teacher has a means for gaining student attention that does not require raising their voice above the student noise level.	**Student Evidence:** • Students demonstrate the ability to follow the teacher directions. • When the teacher signals to gain student attention, the students stop what they are doing and saying.

	Innovating (4.0)	Applying (3.0)	Developing (2.0)	Beginning (1.0)
Structured Small-Group Discussion Protocols	My use of this standard is creative enough to be shared with other faculty members so they can use it with their students.	I use a variety of structured small-group discussion protocols to meet intended instructional objectives.	I attempt to use structured small-group discussion protocols, but the results of my attempts are frequently ineffective.	I have made minimal effort to structured small-group discussion protocols.

Based on your score, create a goal for improving in the use of structured small-group discussion protocols. Make your goal specific, measurable, realistic, and time-bound. For example, *I will achieve the applying level of using structured small-group discussion protocols by the date of my annual summative review.* Next, describe the specific action steps you will take to reach this goal and evidence you will use to demonstrate goal attainment.

Small-group discussion protocols profile				
Small-group discussions	*Rating*			
	Innovating	*Applying*	*Developing*	*Beginning*
Structured Small-Group Discussion Protocols.				
Based on my profile, my goal is to:				
To achieve this goal, I will:				
I know that I will have achieved this goal when:				

This chapter has provided teachers with a variety of structured small-group protocols for student discussion. The next chapter focuses on implementing student-led small-group discussions. Student-led small-group discussions are less structured thus shifting the majority of the discussion responsibility to the students.

Chapter 4

Student-Led Small-Group Discussions

The traditional small-group student-led discussion is less structured than all of the protocols presented in the prior chapter. The fact that it is less structured than the formats previously presented also makes it more flexible. Any whole-class discussion topic can be used with a structured small-group format. The main difference is that students, not the teacher, assume ownership of the discussion.

When planning for and implementing student-led small-group discussions, the five-step cycle described for teacher-guided discussions that was presented in chapter 2 remains the same with the following exceptions.

- With student-led small-group discussions, advance thought must be given to both the size and the composition of groups.
- When using student-led small-group discussions, advance thought must be given to assigning student roles and responsibilities.
- It is necessary for the teacher to establish routines unique to the format.
- During student-led small-group discussions, the role of the teacher changes.
- In student-led small-group discussions, the focus of reflection shifts from whole-class to small-group processes.

STUDENT-LED SMALL-GROUP DISCUSSIONS

Group size and composition

The structured small-group protocols specify the size of the group. What should be the size of a group when conducting student-led small-group discussions? The size of groups for these discussions should remain between three and five students. A minimum of three students is necessary to form a group (otherwise you have a pair). A maximum of five members make it more likely that every group member will need to actively participate while at the same time avoiding the sense of feeling overwhelmed or disconnected. Groups consisting of more than five members encourage the formation of subgroups and side-conversations. In addition, it is common in larger groups for some individuals to put forth minimal effort while others do the majority of the work.

Teachers of students with minimal experience participating in small-group discussions should strive for groups of three. This is also the case with teachers of both primary age students and students who demonstrate low levels of discussion skills. When considering formation of the composition of these groups, it depends upon the age and experience level of the students.

There are three main approaches to forming student-led discussion groups, each of which has pros and cons. The first approach to forming these groups is for the teacher to decide who will be in each one. This approach is efficient, reduces potential student disagreements and hurt feelings, and allows the teacher to balance teams for maximum effectiveness. If you know students well enough, you can balance characteristics such as big-picture and detail-oriented thinkers or introverts and extroverts. In addition, this approach is authentic as most teams in the world outside of school do not have the opportunity to self-select. Outside of the school setting, students need to learn to work with a diversity of people. On the other hand, some students may be disgruntled about their team composition and may lose a sense of ownership of and buy-in for the discussion process.

A second approach is for the teacher to make the final decision regarding group composition after receiving student input. This approach minimizes disagreements and hurt feelings while still allowing the teacher to balance groups for maximum effectiveness. In addition, students will retain a sense of ownership and buy-in while having the opportunity to learn to choose teammates wisely. This approach takes more teacher time. Also, because it can be difficult to honor all students' preferences, some students are still likely to be disgruntled about their group composition.

The final approach to group composition is for the teacher to manage the process of students' making the decision. Because of their involvement in the decision-making process, student disagreements are minimized and the sense of ownership and buy-in for the discussion process is increased. However, this approach takes more classroom time and has significant potential for hurting the feelings of some students. It is not advised to use this approach with either very young or socially immature students. In addition, the classroom culture needs to be right in order to prevent issues with cliques and socially marginalized students.

The ideal approach is to balance teacher-created discussion groups with student-selected ones. This will provide some opportunities for students to connect socially with their friends while also stretching their collaborative skills and providing exposure to varied viewpoints. Regardless of the method used, the teacher must strive to have students work with as many different peers as possible over the course of the school year.

Roles and responsibilities

Within traditional small-group discussions, it is desirable to assign or have students select roles. These roles are not necessary and are sometimes counterproductive for the structured protocols presented previously.

In student-led small-group discussions, task-oriented group roles provide an additional layer of self-management. In turn, these roles help groups run both more effectively and efficiently. With carefully planned and explained roles established, teachers are likely to spend less time working out issues within groups that are not functioning effectively.

All assigned roles must have clearly defined responsibilities. While there are many possible roles for student-led small-group discussion, the following are the most common:

Recorder

- Documents small-group responses in the format required for the discussion activity.
- Takes notes as necessary.
- Shares responses with the Reporter.

Reporter

- Presents group responses to the class.

Time Keeper

- Assists with time management, including keeping the rest of the group aware of the amount of time remaining.

* *Teachers often assume the role of warning students how much time is remaining. This does not encourage student development of time management skills. In addition, teachers often add additional time to discussions. When this happens, students come to realize that the time initially stated is not the real time allotted. Students will not work efficiently if the teacher continuously adds more time for group discussions. Unless there has been a severe, universal miscalculation of time required, do not add more time for task completion.*

Materials Manager

- Organizes/distributes all materials used and returns those materials to the appropriate place.
- Collects work and places it in the appropriate location.

Note that none of these roles place responsibility for behavior expected of all students on one student. When social roles like the encourager or praiser are assigned, we are placing responsibility for a behavior that is desirable for all students to demonstrate onto one student. This type of role sends the wrong message.

Another role that is frequently assigned to groups is that of the questioner. There is a better way to handle questions during group discussions. Teach students the following routine for group questions:

1. If a group member has a question, they must first ask the rest of the group.
2. If no one in the group can answer the question, then all group members must raise their hand.
3. Seeing all hands raised, the teacher will move to that group. Upon arriving, the teacher will select any of the group members to ask the question.
4. If the student selected does not know the group's question, the teacher shall prompt students to discuss it again and come back when every group member is capable of asking the question. If the selected student knows the question, the teacher answers it.

This process of requiring group questions eliminates wasted teacher time. Frequently a student in the group already knows the answer to a question an individual student would have asked the teacher.

Teacher role during student-led small-group discussions

In the teacher-guided discussions explained in chapter 2, the teacher is the person primarily responsible for sustaining the discussion through their use of modeling, scaffolding and coaching. In the structured small-group discussion protocols described earlier in this chapter, the protocols themselves scaffold and sustain the discussion. In student-led groups, the students themselves assume responsibility for the discussion.

This doesn't mean the teacher has no role to play. In student-led small-group discussions, the teacher assumes the role of the monitor and supporter. As a monitor the teacher takes notes of student progress relating to the application of focus skills. These notes can be used when reflecting on group processes and may serve as inspiration for future mini-lessons. In addition, he or she monitors student understanding of content, stepping in to correct misunderstandings only after providing other students the opportunity to make the correction. Lastly, in their role as a monitor, the teacher makes sure students are completing the responsibilities associated with any assigned group roles.

As a discussion supporter, the teacher is responsible for interacting with groups when necessary. Sometimes small discussion groups get bogged down or get completely off topic. When this happens, the teacher provides a scaffold designed to move the discussion forward toward the desired outcomes. Usually, this takes the place of a question or statement designed to prompt students to take a different course of action. For example, with a group that has gotten off-topic, the teacher might say, "while those are interesting points you are making, I am wondering how they relate to our discussion topic?" Another example is when the content of a discussion has devolved into unsubstantiated opinions the teacher might say, "I find myself wondering what evidence from the text you have for that statement?" These types of statements bring the issue to the group's awareness and prompt them to change course.

As a supporter, we must always encourage students to accept responsibility for the discussion. Sometimes this means letting go of control and not being in charge. It is tempting to intervene as soon as a group appears to be off course. However, we must allow time and opportunities for students to learn and practice the skills of managing the process. Given time and opportunities, it is often surprising how well students can manage the discussion process on their own. This is especially true when they have had significant experience with teacher-guided discussions and mini-lessons on communication and reasoning skills. Err on the side of patience when supporting student-led small-group discussions.

Processing group and individual performance

In teacher-guided discussions, the focus for reflection is on individual and whole class performance. In small-group discussions, the focus still includes individual performance but replaces whole-class performance with that of the group. Processing of performance is not always necessary when using the structured protocols. This is especially true when they are being used briefly as part of direct instruction related to content.

When protocols are used for extended periods of time and require significant levels of student interaction, it is appropriate to incorporate opportunities for processing of performance. It is also always appropriate to provide structured opportunities for reflection in student-led small-group discussions.

The purpose of group processing is reflection and then discussion of how well students are achieving their goals and maintaining effective working relationships. Groups need to describe what member actions are helpful and unhelpful and make decisions about what behaviors to continue or change. Continuous improvement of the process of learning results from the careful analysis of how members are working together.

In order to process both individual and group performance, the teacher can provide the following prompts:

- What did I do well as a member of this group?
- What could I do better as a group member in the future?
- What did our group do well?
- What changes could be made to improve the quality of future group work?

Students then individually write responses to each of these questions. After providing adequate time for the recording of responses, teachers prompt students to share their answers for the group performance. Going clockwise starting with a designated student, each group shares one thing their group did well. After all students have had their turn, the process is repeated with the sharing of one change the group could make to improve the quality of future group work.

After every group member has had the opportunity to share, the teacher can share his or her observations. It is best to keep these observations focused at the group level, not singling out any specific student. If desired, a whole-class discussion can ensue. Lastly, teachers collect the student responses reviewing those focused on individual performance. Individual responses offer valuable information about student's needs and thoughts regarding the discussion process.

SELF-RATING OF STUDENT-LED SMALL-GROUP DISCUSSIONS

How do I use student-led small-group discussions to achieve instructional objectives?	
The teacher uses student-led small-group discussions to meet instructional objectives.	
Teacher Evidence:	**Student Evidence:**
• The size and composition of the groups facilitate meeting the instructional objective.	• Students demonstrate acceptance of group members.
• Group roles and responsibilities have been clearly explained and assigned.	• Students demonstrate understanding of their roles by completing the assigned responsibilities.
• The teacher demonstrates appropriate skills for handling group questions.	• Students only ask the teacher a question when all of the students in their group do not know the answer.

- The teacher only intervenes in small-group discussions when necessary.
- When intervening in a small group, the teacher keeps the responsibility for the discussion with the students.
- The teacher provides structured opportunities for reflection on individual and group performance.
- The teacher analyzes information collected from reflection activities to plan for future student-led small-group discussions.
- Students complete the discussion task assigned by the teacher.
- Students conduct a thoughtful, honest appraisal of both individual and group performance related to discussion skills.

	Innovating (4.0)	Applying (3.0)	Developing (2.0)	Beginning (1.0)
Discussion Closure	My use of this standard is creative enough to be shared with other faculty members so they can use it with their students.	I use student-led small-group discussions that meet my instructional objectives.	I attempt to use student-led small-group discussions, but the results of my attempts are frequently ineffective.	I have made minimal effort to use student-led small-group discussions.

SELF-RATING SUMMARY AND PERSONAL GOAL SETTING FOR GROWTH

Directions: Based on the aforementioned score, select a goal for improving in the use of student-led small-group discussions. Make your goal specific, measurable, realistic, and time-bound. For example, *I will achieve the applying level of using student-led small-group discussion protocols by the date of my annual summative review.* Next, describe the specific action steps you will take to reach this goal and evidence you will use to demonstrate goal attainment.

Small-group discussion protocols profile				
Small-group discussions	Rating			
	Innovating	Applying	Developing	Beginning
Student-Led Small-Group Discussions				
Based on my profile, my goal is to:				
To achieve this goal, I will:				
I know that I will have achieved this goal when:				

Chapters 3 and 4 have described small-group discussion strategies. Mastery of these two types of small-group discussions will enable the teacher to facilitate deep learning of content while also preparing students for life outside of school. Another strategy for facilitating deep learning and preparing students for their future is the use of project-based tasks. Designing, implementing and evaluating project-based tasks is the subject of chapter 5.

Chapter 5

D.E.E.P. Learning Tasks

An educational strategy that has received a great deal of attention among educators is problem-based learning. The core idea of problem-based learning is real-world problems capture students' interest and promote critical thinking skills as students acquire and apply knowledge to authentic problem-solving contexts (David, 2008). When using this strategy, the teacher plays the role of the facilitator, working with students to create worthwhile questions and structure meaningful tasks. In addition, he or she coaches students in the development and application of skills as well as assessing learning. Advocates of this approach state that problem-based learning prepares students for the thinking and collaborations skills required for success in the world outside of school (Barron & Hammond, 2008).

It is true that this learning strategy has several important potential benefits for students. However, there are two main problems with how this strategy has been traditionally implemented. First, problem-based learning has frequently been used as the entry point for instruction. When problem-based learning is used as the method for students to discover knowledge, three negative possibilities can occur.

First, only the brightest and most prepared students might make the desired discovery. Second, many students will become frustrated and give up on finding the solution. Novice learners can engage in discovery learning for extended periods of time and learn almost nothing. Third, students may believe they have discovered a solution but they are incorrect. As a result, they learn misconceptions that can interfere with later learning.

Considering the potential value of problem-based learning and the risks associated with using it as a tool for discovery learning, it is not a question of if students should engage in these activities but where in the learning cycle these activities should occur.

Teachers should provide explicit, direct instruction when introducing a topic. As students demonstrate mastery of declarative knowledge and procedural skills, teachers should introduce complex tasks requiring them to process and integrate what they have learned. As part of the learning cycle, students need opportunities to move beyond the surface level toward deeper learning and long-term retention of content. This is especially true for content likely to be used by students in their future.

The second issue with problem-based learning is the variety of interpretations for what defines a quality project. Projects vary greatly in the depth of questions explored, clarity of learning goals, content and structure of the activity, and the amount of guidance provided by teachers (David, 2008). Without explicit quality standards, it is impossible for problem-based learning activities to be designed and implemented effectively. With the quantity of curriculum to be taught and the length of time allowed for that instruction, teachers can ill afford to spend blocks of time on tasks that do not promote a clear learning purpose and desired student outcomes.

A master teacher is one that can design and implement high-quality, cognitively complex learning tasks. In addition, he or she knows when and how often to implement these tasks within the learning cycle. This chapter will define "D.E.E.P." learning tasks and explain why, when, and for whom they should be used. In addition, clear criteria for designing these tasks will be provided. Lastly, this chapter will provide teachers with strategies for effectively implementing these types of tasks in their classrooms and assessing the quality of student work.

Definition A "D.E.E.P." learning task is one in which individual or groups of students apply essential declarative knowledge and procedural skills to create a product or performance that addresses an authentic dilemma. Careful reading of this definition reveals there are many decisions a teacher must make in order to design a "D.E.E.P." learning task. These decisions are represented by each letter in the acronym "D.E.E.P."

- **D:** Dilemma. What problem, question, or task will I ask students to solve, answer, or complete?
- **E:** Engagement. How will I make the task as authentic as possible?
- **E:** Equip. What strategies do I need to teach and what materials do I need to provide?
- **P:** Product or Performance. What product or performance are students required to complete?

Well-meaning teachers sometimes believe that these types of tasks are only appropriate for advanced learners. In the name of differentiation, these types of tasks are assigned to one group of students while other students complete work at a lower level of complexity. This is a mistake that often contributes to a widening learning gap between students. All students can benefit from and are capable of higher-order thinking (Brookhart, 2014). Of course, additional supports may be necessary, but all students should complete D.E.E.P. learning tasks.

RATIONALE FOR D.E.E.P. LEARNING TASKS

D.E.E.P. learning tasks are effective means for developing student's critical thinking skills, promoting the transfer of new learning and enhancing the long-term retention of knowledge. There are two aspects of critical thinking that are especially pertinent to D.E.E.P. learning tasks.

First, critical thinking includes the ability to use logical reasoning for creating and supporting arguments. According to Barron and Hammond (2008), students who participate in problem-based experiences are better able to support their claims with well-reasoned arguments. However, exposure to problem-based experiences is insufficient to promote the ability to support reasoning with clear arguments. Developing claims and supporting them with evidence and reasoning requires combining direct instruction with opportunities for application (Goodwin, 2017).

Second, critical thinking includes the ability to examine one's own beliefs and when necessary being able to change them in light of new, compelling data. Students who complete problem-based experiences demonstrate significant gains in conceptual understanding (Barron & Hammond, 2008). Thus, they are better equipped to make strategic decisions about the ways in which they want to process information and apply that information to a range of complex problems or situations. Once again, this benefit is only realized when the skills required to do this are taught explicitly and then applied to course content. Critical thinking skills do not develop through osmosis.

One of the primary goals of formal education is the transfer of learning from one context or with one set of materials to another context or related set of materials. We do not teach addition solely for students to complete problems in the classroom. Instead, we teach additional skills so eventually students will be able to use this content to solve problems outside of school.

There is abundant evidence demonstrating that this desired outcome of transfer of learning does not occur (Perkins & Salomon, 1992). In part, this is due to the fact that typically the context of the original learning differs significantly from the ultimate contexts for application. It is a far different context to apply a skill through typical classroom tasks than to apply it to the types of work done in the world outside of school.

When designed correctly, problem-based experiences directly engage learners in approximations of the desired performance. Approximations of new learning to the desired future performance context increases both the students' ability and likelihood of using that learning in similar future contexts.

Another goal of instruction is long-term retention of knowledge and skills. Simply put, we want students to retain and be able to recall that which was taught. According to Wolfe (2010), many of our strongest neural networks are formed by actual experience. Problem-based experiences take advantage of this natural proclivity by engaging students in solving authentic problems in their school or community. Authentic problems may not be easy to solve, but it is through this struggle that students may achieve long-term retention of knowledge and skills.

In sum, problem-based experiences containing the characteristics of the D.E.E.P. learning tasks described in the remainder of this chapter promote two important aspects of critical thinking, encourage positive transfer of learning, and increase the probability of long-term retention of content. Having defined D.E.E.P. learning tasks, establishing where in the learning cycle they should occur and with whom, and providing the rationale for using these types of tasks, we now turn to teacher planning for implementation.

ESSENTIAL PRIOR KNOWLEDGE

Before students engage with most D.E.E.P. learning tasks, they must have the ability to develop an argument. If students do not have the capacity to develop an argument, then the teacher must provide age-appropriate, explicit instruction on how to do so. An argument is a conclusion or belief (also known as a claim) supported by evidence. When developing an argument, the goal is to change people's point of view or persuade people to a particular action or behavior. There are four types of claims, which sometimes overlap. They are as follows:

- Claims of cause and effect: Argument that one person, thing, or event caused something else to occur.
- Claims of definition or fact: Argument of what a definition is or if something accepted as fact is really so.
- Claims about values: Argues the worth of something and whether we value it or not.
- Claims about solutions or policies: Argues for or against specific approaches to problems.

Effective claims take a clear position on a debatable topic. There is no claim to be made when something is an undisputed fact. In addition, the claim must be narrow enough to be supported effectively within the scope of the argument. For example, the claim that "vaccines play a role in the prevention of disease" is very broad. Which diseases? Which vaccines? What role do they play? However, the claim of "states should require vaccinations for children entering public school" is narrow enough to be supported with evidence.

To be effective, the author of the claim must use supporting evidence that is valid, sufficient, and relevant. Without evidence, an argument is just an opinion. In chapter 2, the types of evidence used to support an argument were described. Evidence is considered defensible if it does not contain the reasoning errors identified in that chapter. When developing their own arguments, students need to apply that information to make sure their evidence is logical, makes sense and supports their claim.

When developing an argument, students must provide enough evidence to cause the audience to take the claim seriously. An argument is strengthened when the evidence comes from multiple sources and multiple types of evidence are provided. In addition, when developing an argument, students must make sure the evidence relates directly to their claim. Quotations and citations from experts in a field as well as the use of credible and trustworthy information sources strengthen an argument.

In addition to establishing a claim and providing evidence, students must explain their reasoning. More specifically, students must explain why they have taken a position. This explanation, sometimes referred to as a warrant, requires connecting how the evidence provided supports their claim. A simple example is as follows:

Claim: You conclude there are dogs nearby.
Evidence: You believe this because you hear barking and howling.
Reasoning: You connect the sounds of barking and howling with dogs.

An additional strategy that strengthens an argument is anticipating and proactively addressing counterarguments and qualifiers. By acknowledging and understanding opposing viewpoints, the author can explain why their claim holds up despite potential counterarguments. The same is true for identifying and addressing information that serves as non-examples of the claim. Proving you are aware of exceptions makes it more difficult for your audience to believe you do not have a thorough understanding of the topic of the argument. A counterargument for the aforementioned example is that even though other animals bark and howl, dogs are the ones most frequently found in your neighborhood.

A simple outline that can be used to teach students how to produce a written argument is the following.

- Introduction: Introduce your claim.
- Body Paragraph #1: Present your first point and supporting evidence.

- Body Paragraph #2: Present your second point and supporting evidence.
- Body Paragraph #3: Present your third point and supporting evidence.
- Body Paragraph #4: Address counterarguments and qualifiers
- Conclusion: Restate your claim.

Once students are capable of using age-appropriate skills to identify a claim, support that claim with evidence, provide reasoning to connect evidence to the claim, and consider counterarguments, the teacher can design and implement D.E.E.P. learning tasks. The starting point is determination of the content knowledge and skills the dilemma will address.

DILEMMA CONTENT

"D.E.E.P." learning tasks have tremendous potential for engaging students and increasing understanding. However, skill is required when deciding the content of these tasks. Too often, teachers design activities that are supposed to be fun for students without considering the learning we expect students to gain from the task.

For example, I once witnessed a group of elementary age students spend a week of class time constructing tepees as part of a unit on local Native American history. While this task was fun and engaging for students, it ignored the fact that in this case, the local Native American tribes primarily lived in pit houses and brush shelters. This activity took a significant chunk of instructional time to accomplish something that was not even in the curriculum.

"D.E.E.P." learning tasks must be a means to enhance learning and not an end in themselves. These tasks must relate directly, not superficially, to clearly defined curriculum objectives and learning standards. Two factors will help a teacher decide if the objectives and standards are appropriate for this type of task.

The first factor for identifying curriculum standards and learning objectives appropriate for "D.E.E.P." learning tasks is future use. Teachers need to ask themselves, "What is the benefit of this content for use in other classes, at other grade levels and in life outside of school?" Learning how to conduct research and identify credible sources is a skill that is used in many disciplines, at all grade levels and in real-world applications. On the other hand, correctly identifying dates of events or names of historical figures is only useful in select situations. Therefore, if the content will have a high degree of future use in a variety of settings, it is appropriate for "D.E.E.P." learning tasks.

The second factor to consider is the level of cognition required. There are four types of "D.E.E.P." learning tasks. The four types of tasks are categorized as judgment, speculation, problem-solving, or invention. Judgment tasks require thought at the evaluation level of Bloom's Taxonomy. Speculation, problem-solving, and invention tasks require thought at the creation level of Bloom's taxonomy. Thus, if the content does not require thought at these levels, then it is not appropriate for a "D.E.E.P." learning task.

Throughout the remainder of this chapter, a sample task will be described. This sample task is designed for middle school students and is interdisciplinary. It is similar to a real issue confronted by a school. The task described is the culminating task for a unit of instruction. The team of teachers responsible for creating this unit selected the following standards as the focus for instruction. Students will demonstrate the ability to:

- use knowledge of scale drawings to solve a real-life problem;
- solve a real-world problem involving the four operations;
- construct a scientific argument based on evidence for how environmental and genetic factors affect the growth and survival of organisms;
- draw evidence from informational texts to support analysis, reflection, and research;
- gather relevant information from multiple print and digital sources, using search terms effectively; and
- examine land use proposals and make recommendations to the appropriate authority regarding the best course of action.

The task presented throughout the remainder of this chapter is intended to exemplify one possibility. As long as the task meets the "D.E.E.P." criteria, it does not matter if it includes content from one discipline or multiple disciplines. Furthermore, the task can be designed to be completed in a single class period or over an extended period of time. Lastly, the task can be completed in class, independently or some combination of both. All of these decisions depend upon the curriculum, time available, and needs of the students.

DECISION #1—WHAT CONTENT I AM RESPONSIBLE FOR TEACHING HAS A HIGH PROBABILITY OF FUTURE USE BY STUDENTS AND IS AT THE EVALUATE OR CREATE LEVEL OF BLOOM'S TAXONOMY?

Task type and amount of structure

There are four types of tasks. In the following chart, the tasks are defined. In addition, common verbs synonymous with the type of task and a sample task prompt are provided. The type of task selected will depend upon the desired instructional outcomes. For example, if the content standard calls for critiquing a work of art based on specific aesthetic elements, then it is a judgment task. If the content standard requires constructing an argument with evidence that some organisms cannot survive in a specific type of habitat, that would be an invention task.

Task Type	Definition	Synonymous Verbs	Sample Prompt
Judgment	Tasks requiring students to make considered decisions or come to sensible conclusions.	Critique, appraise, assess, decide, conclude, rate	Decide which of the following is more important and provide rationale supporting your choice.
Problem-solving	Tasks requiring students to find solutions to difficult problems or complex issues.	Investigate, resolve, devise, conceive, determine	Devise a solution to _____. Explain why you think your solution would work.
Speculation	Tasks requiring students to form a theory or conjecture based on available evidence.	Predict, hypothesize, theorize, conjecture	Predict what might have happened if _____. Explain how you reached your conclusion.
Invention	Tasks requiring students to create a unique or novel device, method, composition, or process.	Create, construct, design, develop, devise	Develop a process for _____. Explain why your process would resolve the problem presented.

The following are examples of each type of task:

- **Judgment**
    o Should zoos exist? Why or why not?
    o Should the U.S. government allow immigrants here illegally to become U.S. citizens? Why or why not?
    o Is kneeling down during the national anthem an appropriate form of protest? Why or why not?

- **Problem-Solving**
    o Some parents demand that the book *The Handmaid's Tale* be banned from the school curriculum. School faculty believe that it is a classic that must be taught. How might you resolve this dilemma?

- o   Social media often consists of misinformation that is presented as fact. Devise a solution for correcting this problem.
- o   Water bottles made of plastic are creating an environmental hazard. A group of concerned citizens wants to ban them in your community. Yet, we want people to drink sufficient amounts of water and many people use them. Devise a solution to the problem.

- **Speculation**
  - o   Can alternative energy sources effectively replace fossil fuels? Why or why not?
  - o   Does expanding nuclear energy contribute to the proliferation of nuclear weapons? Why or why not?
  - o   What might happen if the voting age was lowered to sixteen? How do you know?

- **Invention**
  - o   Create a way for someone using crutches to carry small personal items.
  - o   Develop a method that results in people using less water every day.
  - o   Construct something that would result in less animals being hit by cars.

When designing these tasks, features can be adjusted to provide various amounts of structure. More specifically, the dilemma, the selection and use of strategies and materials, and the required final product can all be either more or less structured. On the one extreme, the task feature is decided by the student. On the other extreme, the feature is provided by the teacher. A medium amount of structure is provided when the teacher guides the students in decision-making related to the tasks feature. These teacher decisions are represented in the following table.

Task feature	Low structure	Medium structure	High structure
Dilemma	Not provided	Teacher-guided student decision.	Teacher provided
Selection of strategies and materials	Not provided	Teacher-guided student decision	Teacher provided
Final product	Not provided	Teacher-guided student decision	Teacher provided

When making decisions regarding the amount of structure a teacher will provide, he or she must consider the age and abilities of the students. Younger students, and those with less experience completing these types of tasks, will require higher amounts of structure. Older, more experienced, more skilled students will require lower levels of structure.

Varying the amount of structure provided is an example of differentiating instruction. However, if we vary the amount of structure without deliberate consideration of the desired learning outcome, we can make the task invalid. For example, if the desired outcome is for students to independently select a strategy for solving a problem, then the teacher cannot assign the strategies required for task completion. If the desired outcome is for students to independently select appropriate sources for research, then the teacher cannot provide sources.

Due to disabilities or limited language proficiency, some students may require extensive structure to complete the task. If the level of structure changes the nature of the task to the extent it no longer reflect the desired learning outcomes, the teacher must be clear in communicating that fact when making summative judgments of performance.

DECISION #2: WHAT TYPE OF TASK IS MOST APPROPRIATE FOR REACHING DESIRED STUDENT OUTCOMES AND HOW MUCH/WHAT TYPE OF STRUCTURE WILL STUDENTS REQUIRE TO COMPLETE IT?

Engagement

For most students, motivation to complete a task will be high if it involves real-world applications. In addition, if the task enables students to make an impact on the world, and/or speaks to students' personal concerns or interests, they will put forth additional effort to generate a quality product. With the goal of promoting student engagement, teachers designing a D.E.E.P. learning task must strive for authenticity.

To promote authenticity, the teacher shall provide a task description including the role the student is to play, the context for the problem, and the audience for the product or performance. In particular, knowing the audience helps students to shape the tone, content, and style of their final product. Creating a performance for elementary-age students is very different from creating one for a group of local business professionals.

Sometimes these aspects of the task description can be real, other times the best we can do is provide an imagined scenario. However, as a general rule, the more authentic the task, the more engaging it is for students. Whenever possible, strive to address real-world problems in your school and community.

To develop a task description requires the teacher to answer the following three questions:

- Who uses this knowledge or skill in the world outside of the classroom? (role)

- Where and when do they use this knowledge or skill? (context)
- Who are the typical recipients of these work products? (audience)

The answers to these three questions commonly form the introduction of the task description. The following example highlights the blending of context, role, and audience to introduce an engaging D.E.E.P. learning task.

Approximately twenty years ago, a principal named Mr. Rose passed away. In his honor, the school built a "Rose Garden" in one of the courtyards. Over the years, this garden has not been properly maintained. As a result, it is overgrown, filled with weeds, and has several dead bushes. Mr. Rose's niece has donated $500 to the school P.T.A. to restore this memorial (Context). *Her single request was that students must be involved in completing the task* (Role). *The P.T.A. grant committee has decided they will award the money to the class that develops the best proposal for completing the project* (Audience).

Note that this part of the task description is highly structured. It identifies a specific context, role, and audience, all of which are provided by the teacher. A less structured approach could have simply asked students to select a problem in their school they could address given a $500 budget.

DECISION #3: WHAT IS THE CONTEXT, ROLE, AND AUDIENCE THAT WILL BE DESCRIBED IN AN EFFORT TO ENGAGE STUDENT MOTIVATION?

Product or performance

While out of order with the acronym for "D.E.E.P.," the type of product or performance is the next decision. Without knowing the final product or performance required, it is not possible to equip students with the appropriate materials and strategies.

If the task is to serve as a valid measure of student learning, the type of final product required cannot conflict with the essential desired student outcomes. For example, if the objective is for students to produce a five-paragraph essay, then they cannot produce a final product that is a drawing. On the other hand, if the final product must only represent understanding of specific content, then students choice for representing this knowledge can vary. In this case, it would not matter if the product was a diagram, video, or essay. Alignment between the product required and the outcomes desired is essential.

Another aspect of the desired end product or performance that deserves special consideration is who will complete it. More specifically, will the task be completed by a group, will it be done individually, or will it be some combination of the two? Students working together in a group small enough that everyone can participate meaningfully on a collective task have significant learning benefits (Barron & Hammond, 2008). Research has repeatedly demonstrated that teams outperform individuals on all types of problems across all age groups (Johnson & Johnson, 1989).

On the other hand, completion of group products does not enable teachers to make judgments on individual learners' performance. Thus, if students work together on part of the task, it is important that they still complete an individual product or performance. This is the only way to determine if the student has achieved the desired learning outcome.

A combined approach allowing students to work together on a part of the task but then complete an individual product is often the best design. Ultimately, the decision on whether students should work together or not will depend on the content, the needs of the learners, and the outcomes sought.

Continuing the example of the "Rose Garden" provided in the previous section, the following is a sample description for a product or performance. This description would come after the introduction.

The proposal for the grant must include the following items:

1. *A scale drawing demonstrating the layout of the garden. It is an eight-foot wide by ten-foot-long plot of land. This plot receives approximately four hours of direct sunlight daily.*
2. *A detailed budget for the items that includes the quantity, description, and cost for each item or service that must be purchased. Keep in mind the following factors when developing the budget:*
   a. *The custodial crew has agreed that they will remove all of the current plants and debris.*
   b. *The school district is a tax-exempt organization.*
   c. *The soil quality is adequate.*
   d. *This plot of land has no current source of irrigation.*
   e. *Any tools required for completing the project can be borrowed.*

For any living items you choose to include in your budget, provide a separate description for why those items are appropriate for this environment.
3. *A description of 500 words or less for how this garden will reflect Mr. Rose's belief that all children can learn and grow, but not in the same way and not at the same time.*

Note that this description contains the key parameters a student must consider when creating the final product or performance. This description is an example of providing a medium amount of structure for the final product or performance. The teacher has provided important guidance, but has allowed for several aspects of student decision-making.

DECISION #4: WHAT PRODUCT OR PERFORMANCE WILL STUDENTS PROVIDE THAT DEMONSTRATES PROFICIENCY WITH THE INTENDED LEARNING OUTCOME(S)?

Equipping students with materials and strategies

Another aspect of designing a D.E.E.P. learning task is determining what unique skills students will need to be taught to complete the task. In addition, the teacher needs to determine the materials and equipment required for task completion.

Obviously, the teacher will need to ensure students have the appropriate content knowledge and skills. This knowledge and skill should have been developed during the preceding unit of instruction. In our example, this includes content such how to create a scale drawing and how to research plant growth needs.

Both judgment and problem-solving tasks benefit from additional explicit instruction on how to use specific cognitive processes. Completing a judgment task requires decision-making skills. A decision-making matrix is a helpful tool for selecting between alternatives. A decision-making matrix is a table that lists criteria vertically and alternatives horizontally. The students then use a numerical rating (weighted if some criteria are more important than others) to assess each alternative. After ranking each alternative, the students decide which one best meets the criteria.

The following is an example of completed decision-making matrix students can be taught to use for making decisions:

Criteria	Alternative 1	Alternative 2	Alternative 3
Cost (x 2)	4	4	6
Feasibility	3	2	2
Sustainability	2	1	3

1 Meets some of the task criteria.
2 Meets most of the task criteria.
3 Meets all of the task criteria.

In this case, alternative #3 would be the best choice. A blank copy of this decision-making matrix is located in the appendix.

A problem-solving task requires problem-solving skills. "S.O.D.A.S." is an acronym describing a structured process students can use to solve a problem. The letters describe the steps in the process.

- **S**: Situation. What is the problem you are being asked to solve?
- **O**: Options. What options can potentially solve this problem?
- **D**: Disadvantages of each option. What are the disadvantages of each option?
- **A**: Advantages of each option. What are the advantages of each option?
- **S**: Solution. Which option best solves the problem?

Sometimes the solution is a combination of the original options. The following is a sample completed graphic organizer. A blank copy is located in the appendix.

Problem-solving organizer		
S: Situation: What is the problem I am being asked to solve? Some students smoke in the bathroom during the school day. How do we stop this from happening?		
O: Options: What alternatives can solve this problem?		
OPTION 1 Install smoke detectors.	OPTION 2 Teach kids about the dangers of smoking.	OPTION 3 Provide students with a smoking cessation program.
D: Disadvantages: What are the disadvantages of each option?		
OPTION 1 Students can blow smoke out the window.	OPTION 2 Learning it does not mean students will apply it.	OPTION 3 Students will not come forward for help because they will be afraid of being disciplined.
A: Advantages: What are the advantages s of each option?		
OPTION 1 Easy and inexpensive.	OPTION 2 Already part of our health curriculum.	OPTION 3 Gets to the root of the problem.
S: Solution: What solution will work best to solve this problem? We will install smoke detectors in the bathroom and make sure the windows in bathrooms are locked.		

In addition to the cognitive skills students may need to be taught, the teacher must give thought to specific materials and equipment students will need. For example, in the task previously described, students will need measurement tools, graph paper, internet access, and so on. This statement comes at the end of the task description. For example:

To complete this project, you will be provided with the following materials:

- *Flyers from the Home Depot and Lowes.*
- *Graph paper*
- *Measurement tools including a ruler, yardstick and tape measure.*
- *Internet access*

If you require any additional materials, please consult with the teacher.

DECISION #5: WHAT STRATEGIES AND RESOURCES WILL MY STUDENTS NEED TO COMPLETE THIS TASK?

The outcomes of all of these decisions are combined to create a clear task description. This written description must be as concise and as clear as possible in order for students to understand the task parameters and required outcomes. The finishing touches for the task description include the evaluation criteria and the deadline for completion.

Assessment

Objective tests are usually appropriate for assessment of declarative and procedural knowledge. This is due to the fact that declarative and procedural knowledge have a single correct answer. By their nature, D.E.E.P. learning tasks have multiple possible answers, each of which can be considered correct if it has the appropriate supporting evidence and reasoning. Therefore, these tasks require a different method of assessment—scoring guides.

A scoring guide is a table consisting of task specific performance factors listed vertically and levels of quality listed horizontally. The performance factors are general categories of significance for completing a quality product. The levels of quality represent qualitative differences in achieving the performance factors.

The levels of qualities are provided along a continuum progressing from a score of 1 for low quality and 4 for quality that exceeds expectations. A score of 3 usually represents meeting the expectations for performance.

Each box in the table represents a description of the performance factor at that level of quality. If they are to be valid, these descriptors must be clearly written statements of the level of expectation for the specific category identified as critical for successful completion of the final product.

When designed correctly and implemented effectively, scoring guides have several key benefits. First, if introduced prior to or near the beginning of assigning the task scoring guides serve as an advance organizer for student work. Students will be aware of the expectations and can execute specific goals as they work to accomplish the task.

Second, if the teacher creates the scoring guide prior to implementing the task, it can serve as an advance organizer for designing instruction. After creating the scoring guide, the teacher will have greater clarity about what the students need to accomplish and can then make instructional decisions accordingly.

Third, if the scoring guide is written with student friendly language, students can use it to self-assess their work. The ultimate goal of assessment should be for students to become critical self-assessors of their own work.

Finally, the teacher can use the scoring guide to provide students with targeted and specific feedback on final products and performances. A quality scoring guide will make it clear to students why they received a particular rating. This feedback can help shape future performances.

It is not possible to provide scoring guides that encompass all of the types of tasks students might complete. Thus, two scoring guides are provided to serve as examples that may be modified to suit specific tasks.

One final note on scoring student work is that if the student's product or performance meets all of the criteria in one level of quality and some of the criteria in the one above it, then it is acceptable to provide a partial score. For example, the student's product represents all of the quality descriptors in level 2 and some of the descriptors in level 3, then a valid score would be a 2.5.

The final statement provided in the task description is how the product or performance will be assessed and if appropriate the deadline for submission. Continuing with the example from this chapter, the following would be the conclusion of the task description:

The grant proposal will be assessed by the committee using the scoring guide attached. The deadline for grant submissions is January 15th.

Critical thinking skills scoring guide

	Score 4.0	Score 3.0	Score 2.0	Score 1.0
Identifying Common Errors in Reasoning	When analyzing information, the student demonstrates the ability to identify errors in logic. In addition, the student can articulate how these errors undermine the position being presented.	When analyzing information, the student demonstrates the ability to identify errors in logic.	The student can describe and/or recognize common logic errors.	The student does not demonstrate the ability to identify common errors in logic.
Generating Conclusions	The student demonstrates the ability to use information in order to generate logical conclusions.	The student demonstrates the ability to examine the validity and truthfulness of conclusions.	The student can describe the characteristics of logical conclusions.	The student does not demonstrate the ability to generate conclusions.
Convergent and Divergent Thinking	The student demonstrates the ability to use convergent and divergent thinking process to independently address complex issues and problems.	The student demonstrates the ability to use convergent and divergent thinking processes to address teacher provided issues and problems.	The student can define convergent and divergent thinking processes.	The student does not demonstrate the ability to use convergent and divergent thinking skills.
Identifying Relationships Between Ideas	The student demonstrates the ability to identify, analyze, and articulate the relationships between ideas.	The student demonstrates the ability to use graphic organizers to identify the relationships between ideas.	The student can identify the relationships between ideas with teacher prompting or assistance.	The student does not demonstrate the ability to identify relationships between ideas.

(Continued)

(Continued)

Service project scoring guide

	Score 4.0	Score 3.0	Score 2.0	Score 1.0
Understanding of Problem or Issue	Student has conducted comprehensive research on the problem or issue and has used that research as a basis for formulating a service-project.	Student has conducted adequate research on the problem or issue and has connected this research to the formulation of the service-project.	Student has conducted limited research on the problem or issue and has attempted to connect the research to the formulation of the service-project.	Student does not demonstrate an understanding of the problem or issue with no evidence of having conducted research.
Application of Knowledge and Skills	Student provides clear evidence of using knowledge and/or skills learned as part of the curriculum to address the problem or issue. The connection is both direct and logical.	Student provides adequate evidence of using knowledge and/or skills learned as part of the curriculum to address the problem or issue.	Student provides limited evidence of using knowledge and/or skills learned as part of the curriculum to address the problem or issue.	Student does not apply knowledge and or skills learned as part of the curriculum to the service project.

Service project scoring guide

	Score 4.0	Score 3.0	Score 2.0	Score 1.0
Impact	Student provides evidence of meaningful contributions to solving a problem or issue. Efforts have the potential to lead to long-term improvements.	Student provides evidence of contributions to solving the problem or issue. The evidence provided demonstrates short-term impact on the problem or issue.	Student provides limited evidence of contributions to solving the problem or issue. The evidence provided demonstrates superficial contributions to improving the problem or issue.	No evidence is provided to the project that has an impact on the problem or situation.
Reflection (Not graded)	Student provides evidence of reflection that shows growth regarding both self in the community and the value of service of others.	Student provides evidence of reflection on the experience. The reflection is limited to the experience and does not include meaningful personal connections.	Student provides limited evidence of reflection on the experience. The reflection is superficial and primarily descriptive in nature.	No evidence of reflection on the experience provided.

DECISION #6: HOW WILL I ASSESS COMPLETED STUDENT WORK?

The six key decisions a teacher must make prior to presenting the D.E.E.P. learning task can be organized using the planning template found in the appendix.

Implementation of D.E.E.P. learning tasks

By far the hardest part of using D.E.E.P. learning tasks is the amount of teacher preparation required. However, a high-quality task can be ruined if the teacher does not effectively perform their role during implementation. When initiating a D.E.E.P. learning task, the teacher should use an entry event, clearly explain the task, and serve as a facilitator of successful task completion.

A teacher can launch the task with an "entry event." This event must be designed to engage student interest and initiate questioning. For example, an entry event can be a guest speaker, a video, a field trip, a piece of real or mock correspondence, or anything else that activates students thinking about the task. The entry event for the task described in this chapter was students serving as the audience for the guest speaker, Mr. Rose's daughter. The students listened to Mr. Rose's daughter describe her father and his career. Subsequently, they asked her questions that arose spontaneously as well as those they prepared in advance.

After the entry event, the teacher must introduce the task. He or she must ensure that all students understand the steps involved in completing the task. This requires provision of the written task description accompanied by a verbal explanation. If available, models of a completed product or performance will make the desired outcomes concrete. The clearer the requirements of the task, the more likely students will achieve the desired goal.

As students engage in completing D.E.E.P. learning tasks, the teacher must be a highly visible, accessible presence in the classroom. He or she should move about the classroom providing assistance as needed while monitoring student work completion. Part of this assistance might be asking guiding questions to encourage higher-level thinking. Assistance may also take the form of providing students with feedback statements designed to guide performance.

Importantly, after the students understand the task, the role of the teacher becomes that of the facilitator for student learning. Students need the opportunity to grapple with these tasks independently. Therefore, the teacher must be intentional about serving as the student's guide and not the leader of learning.

For lengthy tasks involving multiple steps, the teacher may wish to provide students with a checklist. This checklist may include interim deadlines. One advantage of interim deadlines for each step of the task is that the teacher can use them to check in with students as they progress toward task completion. Check-ins are valuable for providing formative feedback to students so they can make any necessary adjustments prior to final submission of their work.

Reflection

All D.E.E.P. learning tasks should conclude with reflection on the content learned and the processes used. For a project that requires only a short time to complete, student reflection can be simple. For example, students can be required to write in their journals the answer to the following two questions:

- What did you learn about _____ as a result of completing this task?
- How effective was the process you used to complete this task? Looking back, would you have done anything differently?

Time permitting, students may be directed to share their responses with a partner.

For extended projects, the reflection might take a more comprehensive format. Perhaps students will need to complete an essay that describes both what they learned and the process used to complete the task. Another option would be for students to complete a portfolio consisting of student selected items. In this case, students could complete a reflection describing the rationale for each item selected.

It is important to be mindful of how you evaluate student reflections. Evaluation of reflections can be counter-productive. It is appropriate to provide feedback on reflections, affirming new realizations and connections students make. It is also appropriate to probe thinking to push students' thinking deeper. At most, a rating should be provided for completely meeting the requirements of the prompt in a thoughtful manner.

Students' reflections can provide powerful data about students' thinking and areas of challenge. This information can then be used by the teacher to revise and improve future task design. Varied forms of reflection with clearly structured prompts are a necessary conclusion to all D.E.E.P. learning tasks.

SELF-RATING ON USE OF D.E.E.P. LEARNING TASKS

Do I effectively design, implement, and evaluate D.E.E.P. learning tasks appropriately?

Teacher Evidence:
- The task description includes appropriate content at the appropriate cognitive level.
- The task description is designed to engage students.
- The task description includes a product or performance matching desired student learning outcomes.
- The teacher ensures students have the necessary prior knowledge and skills for these types of tasks.
- The amount of structure provided for students is appropriate to their abilities and age level.
- The teacher provides instruction in strategies and the necessary resources required for task completion.
- A scoring guide for the task is provided.
- The teacher ensures students understand the task, provides an entry event, and serves as a facilitator of student learning.
- The teacher provides appropriate opportunities for reflection.

Student Evidence:
- Students are motivated to complete the task.
- Students understand the requirements of the task.
- Students are appropriately challenged by the task.
- Students have the knowledge and skills required to complete the task.
- Students can identify what constitutes a quality product or performance.
- Students do the work to complete the task.
- Students reflect thoughtfully on the content learned and the processes used.

	Innovating (4.0)	*Applying (3.0)*	*Developing (2.0)*	*Beginning (1.0)*
D.E.E.P. Learning Tasks	My use of this standard is creative enough to be shared with other faculty members so they can use it with their students.	I effectively design, implement, and evaluate student learning through the use of D.E.E.P. learning tasks.	I attempt to use D.E.E.P. learning tasks, but the results of my attempts are frequently ineffective.	I have made minimal effort to use D.E.E.P. learning tasks with my students.

D.E.E.P. Learning Tasks Profile				
D.E.E.P. Learning Tasks	Rating			
	Innovating	Applying	Developing	Beginning
D.E.E.P. Learning Tasks				
Based on my profile, my goal is:				
To achieve this goal, I will:				
I know that I will have achieved this goal when:				

This chapter has provided teachers with a powerful strategy to promote deep student learning. This strategy requires extensive and thoughtful pre-planning by the teacher. However, the benefit for students is learning how to apply critical thinking skills and content to solving real-world problems. These tasks, when properly designed, will promote high levels of student engagement and enhanced long-term retention of content. While it may require additional work on the part of the teacher, these types of tasks will prepare students to meet the challenges they will face in the future.

Study Guide

Beyond the Early Years is the perfect resource for mid-career teachers to use as part of book study groups. It can be used either by individual teachers or as part of a larger structured professional development program. In the large group setting, teachers can be assigned readings in advance and then join with colleagues to discuss and reflect upon key points. If it is to be used effectively as the text for small-group discussions, several components must be in place.

First, there must be a climate that fosters teachers feeling free and safe to participate in an ongoing exchange of ideas. Teachers in study groups should be discussing ideas, trying them out in their classroom, and then debriefing the results. The best way to understand different classroom activities and structures is to try them for themselves and then talk about how they worked with the students they teach. Establishing norms for conversations in a group and then enforcing those norms will go a long way toward creating this climate.

Second, groups must be kept to a reasonable size. Often the optimal number is between four and eight group members. Groups of this size increase the opportunities for everyone to contribute to the discussion. There are advantages and disadvantages to mixing grade levels and subject areas. More diverse groups will add new perspectives to the conversation and extend the types of applications discussed. Less diverse groups allow for a focus on specific grade level and subject area applications.

When reading the assigned segment of text, readers should annotate important points by underlining, coding, or making margin notes. These annotations can be used to remind group members of questions they have, places where they might want to seek clarification or identification of key points they want to discuss.

Groups must have an agenda that will encourage them to remain focused on the topic. It is normal to have some "settling" time before getting to the task at hand, and groups will occasionally drift off topic. Groups must have an agenda to follow that will limit this off-task discussion. The role of a group leader can be created in order to facilitate the discussion, but it is a role that should be rotated. A possible agenda for seven group meetings is provided. Depending upon resources available and district goals, these meetings can be conducted monthly for one year or spread out over several years.

MEETING #1

Preparation: Read and annotate the introduction.

Agenda:

1. Establish or review norms for participation.
2. Conduct introductions.
3. Discuss the following questions:

    a. What would you say are the most important points presented in these sections of the book?
    b. What content did the author present that you already knew and/or were already doing in your classroom?
    c. What content was presented that was either brand new for you or you thought about in a different way after reading this section?
    d. What ideas or activities presented in this section will you implement in your classroom?

4. Review the reading assignment for the next meeting: Read and annotate the text starting with the start of chapter 2 and ending with the self-rating on preparation for discussions.

MEETING #2

Agenda:

1. Discuss the following questions:

    a. What stood out for you as important in this section of reading?
    b. Did anything in this section of text remind you of something you had learned previously or connect with something you already knew about classroom management?

Study Guide

c. What content was presented that was either brand new for you or you thought about in a different way after reading this section?
d. What ideas or activities presented in this section will you implement in your classroom? Do you anticipate any potential barriers to successful implementation?
e. Does your school district have a scope and sequence for speaking and listening skills for classroom discussions? If so, how is it similar or different? If not, would something like the table provided be useful for teachers?
f. If you completed the self-evaluation activities in this section, what areas did you identify as strengths and what areas did you note as areas for improvement?

2. Review the reading assignment for the next meeting: Read and annotate the text starting with the section "Teacher's Role in the Discussion" and ending with the conclusion of chapter 2.

MEETING #3

Agenda:

1. Discuss the following questions:
   a. What have you tried in your classroom that was based on the content from this section of reading? What were the results?
   b. What were the most important points made in this section of reading?
   c. Did anything in this section of text remind you of something you had learned previously or connect with something you already knew about classroom instruction?
   d. What content was presented that was either brand new for you or after reading this section, you thought about in a different way?
   e. Did any of the information in this section of the reading surprise or confuse you?
   f. How are the teacher-guided discussions presented in this chapter the same and different from those you already have with your students?
   g. If you completed the self-evaluation activities in this section, what areas did you identify as strengths and what areas did you note as areas for improvement?
2. Review the reading assignment for the next meeting: Read and annotate the text of chapter 3.

MEETING #4

Agenda:

1. Discuss the following questions:
   a. What have you tried in your classroom that was based on the content from this section of reading? What were the results?
   b. What stood out to you as particularly important in this section of reading?
   c. Did anything in this section of text remind you of something you had learned previously or connect with something you read in our previous reading assignments?
   d. What content was presented that was either brand new for you or you thought about in a different way after reading this section?
   e. Did any of the information in this section of the reading surprise or confuse you?
   f. Which of the protocols presented in this chapter would be easiest for you to implement? Which would be most difficult?
   g. If you completed the self-evaluation activities in this section, what areas did you identify as strengths and what areas did you note as areas for improvement?
2. Review the reading assignment for the next meeting: Read and annotate the text of chapter 4.

MEETING #5

Agenda:

1. Discuss the following questions:
   a. What have you tried in your classroom that was based on the content from this section of reading? What were the results?
   b. What stood out to you as particularly important in this section of reading?
   c. Did anything in this section of text remind you of something you had learned previously or connect with something you read from our previous reading assignments?
   d. What content was presented that was either brand new for you or you thought about in a different way after reading this section?
   e. Did any of the information in this section of the reading surprise or confuse you?

Study Guide

  f. Do you believe your students currently have the capacity to conduct student-led small-group discussions? Why or why not?

  g. If you completed the self-evaluation activities in this section, what areas did you identify as strengths and what areas did you note as areas for improvement?

2. Review the reading assignment for the next meeting: Read and annotate the text beginning with start of chapter five and concluding with Decision #3.

MEETING #6

Agenda:

1. Discuss the following questions:

   a. What have you tried in your classroom that was based on the content from this section of reading? What were the results?

   b. What stood out to you as particularly important in this section of reading?

   c. Did anything in this section of text remind you of something you had learned previously or connect with something you read from our previous reading assignments?

   d. What content was presented that was either brand new for you or you thought about in a different way after reading this section?

   e. Did any of the information in this section of the reading surprise or confuse you?

   f. Based on what you have read in this chapter thus far, how are D.E.E.P. learning tasks different from and similar to problem-based learning activities?

   g. If you completed the self-evaluation activities in this section, what areas did you identify as strengths and what areas did you note as areas for improvement?

2. Review the reading assignment for the next meeting: Read and annotate the text starting with the section on product and performance and concluding with the remainder of the chapter.

MEETING #7

Agenda:

1. Discuss the following questions:

   a. What have you tried in your classroom that was based on the content from this section of reading? What were the results?

b. What stood out to you as particularly important in this section of reading?
c. Did anything in this section of text remind you of something you had learned previously or connect with something you read from our previous reading assignments?
d. What content was presented that was either brand new for you or you thought about in a different way after reading this section?
e. Did any of the information in this section of the reading surprise or confuse you?
f. D.E.E.P. learning tasks require extensive teacher preparation. Are they worth it? Why or why not?
g. If you completed the self-evaluation activities in this section, what areas did you identify as strengths and what areas did you note as areas for improvement?

Appendix

Mini-lesson planning template	
Grade level:	*Subject:*
Topic:	
CONNECT: Students learn why today's instruction is important to them as discussion participants and how the lesson relates to their prior work. The topic of instruction is stated here.	
TEACH: The teacher gives information about the skill. This information may be provided by giving an explanation, showing examples, or through demonstration.	.
HAVE-A-GO: After teaching the skill, students are given a chance to quickly practice what has been taught or to share what they noticed about the demonstration.	
LINK: The teacher reiterates what has been taught. Students are reminded how this lesson relates to their work in discussions, setting a goal for the use of the skill.	

D.E.E.P. learning task planning template

Decision #1: What content I am responsible for teaching has a high probability of future use by students and is at the evaluate or create level of Bloom's Taxonomy?

Decision #2: What type of task is most appropriate for reaching desired student outcomes and how much/what type of structure will students require to complete it?

Judgment ☐	Speculation ☐	Problem-Solving ☐	Invention ☐
Task feature	Low structure	Medium structure	High structure
Dilemma	Not provided	Teacher-guided student decision	Teacher provided
Selection of strategies and materials	Not provided	Teacher-guided student decision	Teacher provided
Final product	Not provided	Teacher-guided student decision	Teacher provided

Decision #3: What is the context, role, and audience that will be described in an effort to engage student motivation?

Context:

Role:

Audience:

Decision #4: What product or performance will students provide that demonstrates proficiency with the intended learning outcome(s)? How will I describe the requirements for that product or performance so they are clear for students?

Decision #5: What strategies and resources will my students need to successfully complete this task?

Decision #6: How will I assess student performance on this task?

Task description as written for students:

Decision-making matrix			
Criteria	Alternative 1	Alternative 2	Alternative 3

1. Meets some of the project criteria.
2. Meets most of the project criteria.
3. Meets all of the project criteria.

Problem-solving organizer		
S: Situation: What is the problem I am being asked to solve?		
O: Options: What alternatives can I develop to solve this problem?		
OPTION 1	OPTION 2	OPTION 3
D: Disadvantages: What are the disadvantages of each option?		
OPTION 1	OPTION 2	OPTION 3
A: Advantages: What are the advantages of each option?		
OPTION 1	OPTION 2	OPTION 3
S: Solution: What solution will work best to solve this problem?		

References

Abrami, P. C., Bernard, R. M., Borokhosvski, E., Waddington, D. I., Wade, C. A., & Persoon, T. (2015). Strategies for teaching students to think critically: A meta-analysis. *Review of Educational Research, 85*(2), 275–314.

Applebee, A. N. (2003). *The language of literature*. New York: McDougal.

Barron, B. & Darling-Hammond, L. (2008). *Powerful learning: What we know about teaching for understanding*. San Francisco, CA: Jossey-Bass, 2008.

Brookhart, S. M. (2014) *How to design questions and tasks to assess student thinking*. Alexandria, VA: Association for Supervision and Curriculum Development.

Clark, R. E., Kirschner, P.A., & Sweller, J. (2012). Putting students on the path to learning: The case for fully guided instruction. *American Educator*, 6–11. Retrieved from https://www.aft.org/sites/default/files/periodicals/Clark.pdf.

Conley, D. T. (2008). *College Knowledge: What it really takes for students to succeed and what we can do to get them ready*. San Francisco, CA: Jossey-Bass.

Conley, D. T. (2014). *Getting ready for college, careers, and the common core*. San Francisco, CA: Jossey-Bass.

Cotton, K. (1988). *Classroom questioning* (School Improvement Research Series: Research You Can Use, Close-up #5). Portland, OR: Northwest Regional Educational Laboratory.

David, J. L. (2008). What research says about project-based learning. *Educational Leadership, 65*, 80–82.

Goodwin, B. (2014). Research says get all students to speak up. *Educational Leadership, 72*, 82–83.

Goodwin, B. (2017). Research matters: Critical thinking won't develop through osmosis. *Educational Leadership, 74*, 80–81.

Hattie, J. (2008). *Visible learning: A synthesis of over 800 meta-analyses relating to achievement*. Abingdon, UK: Routledge Press.

Hunter, M. (1971). *Teach for transfer*. Thousand Oaks, CA: Corwin Press.

Jennings, M. (2021a). *From first year to first rate: Thriving during the early years of a teaching career*. Lanham, MD: Rowman and Littlefield Publishing.

Jennings, M., (2021b). *Transforming novices into professionals: A systematic and comprehensive approach to teacher induction.* Lanham, MD: Rowman and Littlefield Publishing.

Kamil, M. L., Borman, G. D., Dole, J., Kral, C. C., Salinger T., & Torgensen, J. (2008). *Improving adolescent literacy: Effective classroom and intervention practices.* Washington, DC: Institute for Education Sciences.

Murphy, P. K., Wilkinson, I. A. G., Soter, A. O., Hennessy, M. N., & Alexander, J. F. (2009). Examining the effects of classroom discussion on students' comprehension of text: A meta-analysis. *Journal of Educational Psychology, 101*(3), 740–764.

Perkins, D., & Salomon, G. (1992), *Transfer of learning.* The International Encyclopedia of Education, Second Edition. Oxford, UK: Pergamon Press.

Schmoker, M. (2007). Radically redefining literacy instruction: An immense opportunity. *Phi Delta Kappan, 88*(7) 488–493.

Vogler, K. E. (2008). Asking good questions. *Educational Leadership*, 65. Retrieved from http://www.ascd.org/publications/educational-leadership/summer08/vol65/num09/Asking-Good-Questions.aspx.

Wagner, T. (2010). *The global achievement gap: Why even our best schools don't teach the new survival skills our children need—and what we can do about it.* New York: Basic Books.

Walsh, J. A., & Sattes, B. D. (2005) *Quality questioning: Research-based practice to engage every learner.* Thousand Oaks, CA: Corwin Press.

Walsh, J. A., & Sattes, B. D. (2015). *Questioning for classroom discussion: Purposeful speaking, engaged Listening, deep thinking.* Alexandria, VA: Association for Supervision and Curriculum Development.

Wolfe, P. (2001). *Brain matters: Translating research into classroom practice.* Alexandria, VA: Association for Supervision and Curriculum Development.

About the Author

Matthew J. Jennings is a twenty-eight-year veteran of education. He has served as a superintendent, assistant superintendent, director of human resources, director of student services, supervisor of curriculum and instruction, and a classroom teacher. He earned his master's degree and doctorate in educational administration from Rutgers University. https://jennir3.wixsite.com/drjenningsbooks

www.ingramcontent.com/pod-product-compliance
Lightning Source LLC
Chambersburg PA
CBHW020753230426
43665CB00009B/578